REPLACE YOUR SALARY WITH REAL ESTATE

Published by Grammar Factory Publishing, an imprint of MacMillan Company Limited.

Grammar Factory Publishing
MacMillan Company Limited
25 Telegram Mews, 39th Floor, Suite 3906
Toronto, Ontario, Canada
M5V 3Z1

www.grammarfactory.com

Mangos, Donny
Replace Your Salary with Real Estate / Donny Mangos.

Paperback ISBN 978-1-998756-27-8
eBook ISBN 978-1-998756-28-5

   1. BUS036050 BUSINESS & ECONOMICS / Investments & Securities / Real Estate. 2. BUS036000 BUSINESS & ECONOMICS / Investments & Securities / General. 3. BUS050020 BUSINESS & ECONOMICS / Personal Finance / Investing.

Production Credits
Cover design by Designerbility
Interior layout design by Dania Zafar
Book production and editorial services by Grammar Factory Publishing

Grammar Factory's Carbon Neutral Publishing Commitment
Grammar Factory Publishing is proud to be neutralizing the carbon footprint of all printed copies of its authors' books printed by or ordered directly through Grammar Factory or its affiliated companies through the purchase of Gold Standard-Certified International Offsets.

REPLACE YOUR SALARY WITH REAL ESTATE

DONNY MANGOS

GRAMMAR
FACTORY
— EST? 2013 —

TESTIMONIALS

"Amazing. Captivating. Caught my attention. Refreshed a lot of ideas. Reminded me of mistakes I made, and I can't wait to share this with my daughters and some of our clients."

Jamie Purvis, Co-founder, CEO and
Next Level Business Coach at Be Do Have Movement

"This book is so well written and very easy for me (someone who is not well versed in this content) to digest. I appreciated the casual flow (and humour) throughout the entire book."

Trisha Enriquez, Digital Content Creator,
Blogger and Instagram Personality

"I really enjoyed the book and found it to be valuable. It provides a great overview of real estate investing. I felt your passion!"

Tuan Tran, Top Performing Realtor in Toronto
with Turn Key Realty Team

CONTENTS

INTRODUCTION

Week after week, month after month, and year after year, you've been steadily employed and making a decent wage. Got a promotion last year? Amazing – congratulations! You have been working so hard and waiting for a pay raise, and it's finally come through for you. It must feel amazing; you probably rushed home to your family to spread the wonderful news. If you're still waiting for that raise, hang in there, you tell yourself; it's just a little while until that happens. When that promotion arrives, it will be thrilling!

Some of you may not be up for a pay raise. Uh oh. The company may not have hit targets, and there will not be any raises this year. Maybe next year. It's fine because you have choices, right? You could hang in there a bit longer to see if things improve. You may even decide that you should start to see if there's another job somewhere else that you are better qualified for, which will pay you more. Is your objective to find more money doing the same thing you've been doing?

You may not have noticed (or maybe you've chosen to ignore) that you've been slowly but surely setting a trap for yourself. You've had to give up more than just your time in exchange for that regular paycheque. Have you lost your passion or ambition along with it?

Perhaps, in playing it "safe," you've done something perilous by handing control of your earnings (and potential) over to your employer.

Do you ever get to thinking, "What if?"

What if you left this job and went back to school? What if you left this job and started a new career that's more interesting? What if you left this job and started your own business?

That's a lot of wishful thinking. Could you even imagine turning your life upside down and doing things differently than you are today? How would you pay for your mortgage? Will your new life allow you to be around to pick up the kids from school like your current job does? This is absurd! Let's be real. All of that is too risky. So more often than not, we choose the safe route and fall into the trap of false security. You're not alone.

I was just like you. Burning and earning for a mega-sized company; several of them, in fact. In trying to get ahead by position and salary, I followed the precise path described above. I, too, chose the security and stability of a salary. By playing it safe, I gave all my control and freedom to someone else – who had no real connection to me and no responsibility for me. I was a bit luckier than some. I was still young-ish when I realized what I was doing, and I made an important decision back then to regain full control of my own money and my future.

I made that decision because I had seen at close quarters how the safe path destroys a man, possibly his family, and his financial future and confidence. A colleague much older than me, whom I passed every day on the way to my cubicle, vanished overnight after a lifetime's service to the big insurance company we worked for. He fell victim to outsourcing or downsizing. Completely unexpected. I never did find out his name or what department he worked for. To this day, seventeen years later, the memory of this man haunts me to my core. The hairs on the back of my neck stand up. The tears build in my eyes when I recall that moment when I learned that being a loyal employee doesn't prevent you from losing your job. From that point, the 'safe' option of going to work each day for that steady salary no longer seemed risk-free. I will forever be reminded of the importance of being in control of my own life.

Think about it: not only might your employment suddenly become precarious, but you could get sick or injured or need to give up work to care for someone. You never know what will happen, so you need a plan B that gives you financial independence.

As a business graduate with loads of theoretical and some practical experience as an investor, I knew my future self and family needed to focus on investing for financial independence. So, I gathered knowledge and experience in the many ways to invest. You will have noticed that I ended up in real estate as a salesperson and investor, and there's never been a reason to look back. Most investment options reward the investor in one way. Real estate investing pays in three ways, comes with much less risk and has some amazing tax advantages, as you'll discover in this book. When you package up real estate investing, it's no wonder 90% of the world's millionaires gain their wealth through investing in real estate.

If you stopped working today – regardless of whether you had a say in the matter – could you survive financially? Are you working in a career that you are not passionate about? Perhaps you're trapped by the salary and all the obligations you need to meet. What have you given up in exchange for the salary? Possibly, who you are and the things you love to do.

I wrote *Replace Your Salary with Real Estate* for you. For young professionals starting out, for people who are no longer excited by their career, or for those who have seen loyal, experienced colleagues' lives destroyed as I did, and who already suspect that there might be holes in the salaried safety net. You might feel you have no power, but you can take back power if you change how you understand money. *Replace Your Salary with Real Estate* will lay out practical advice on how to get from dependence to independence in your own life and finances. All you need to start the process are some savings to invest with and the education provided in this book.

This is not a theory book about what may or may not work for you. It is not meant to be a book about money. It's about freedom, control and financial independence. *Replace Your Salary with Real Estate* is a guidebook that will show you the path toward creating a new stream of income large enough to replace your salary. You may even decide to keep working for your current employer. Your power comes from the *choice* to make that decision. That's freedom.

The solution is based on my five-step Replace Method, described in this book:

1. Reflect – look at your finances compared to your goals.
2. Rely – build a team and play to their strengths.
3. React – believe in yourself and have courage.

4. Review – set regular intervals to assess your results.
5. Replace Your Salary or Repeat Until You Do – convert your real estate gains into a steady stream of income that exceeds your salary.

You'll learn how to plan for investing; what type of investments you can and should consider; how and why to build a team around you so that you can outsource the tasks best left to professionals; how to interpret and understand your numbers; and when and how to turn all that you have learned and earned into a nice steady stream of cash to replace your current and future salary.

You can and should outsource tasks that you find tedious or dull, but never outsource the understanding. The Replace Method will give you the confidence to step into an amazing future that includes the bigger you. Once you understand the process, you can be the CEO of your own secret company that delegates tasks, makes a lot of money, and doesn't require your time.

In 2021 – the second year of COVID-19 and the best professional year that my real estate business has had – my real estate investments earned more money than I did. I spent the year help-ing clients, coaching Realtors, driving across my city, negotiating, planning, forecasting, consulting and mediating. My investment properties didn't need to do any of that. Still, they out-earned me. A part of me was certainly upset, of course, because I lost the ultimate battle against myself! The things I owned earned more than I did, a fully functioning adult, in a year. I'm still going to consider this a win overall.

My mentor, Jamie Purvis, and I met one day, and he asked me what I wanted to be successful: to live without money problems and buy back my time. The question was, "How much salary do you need to replace so that you can do the things you want to do most?"

Me: $20,000 in passive income per month.

Jamie: How long will it take you to get there?

Me: Ten years if I follow my plan.

Jamie: Cool. Can you do it in five?

Me: Hmm. You know what, I think I can.

Five years later, in 2021, my real estate investment earnings exceeded my job salary. They will do so again every year.

Replace Your Salary with Real Estate will tell you how I did it and how you can do it too. Are you up for the ride of a lifetime?

PART ONE:

THE HOUSE
ALWAYS WINS

1

THE BASICS OF INVESTING

There are two major ways you can make money in our world. You can work for it (where you trade your time for someone else's money), or you can have your money make you more money. The second way is commonly referred to as investing.

One of my favourite quotes is from J.L. Collins, who wrote in *The Simple Path to Wealth*: "Money can buy many things, but nothing more valuable than your freedom." That's what this entire process is about. It's not about the money; it's about the freedom you'll discover when you conquer the money goal – freedom of time, money and relationships.

When you have the income part sorted, the mind works on the things that energize and excite you. That's what we're after.

Where do we start? In a kind of abstract way, the path to wealth begins with security and control. It would help if you felt safe first before you could truly build. Only when we have removed the risk we associate with our incomes can we see growth from within. We intuitively know that what we think is safe money (job income) is rarely safe. It's a false security, which is why most of us don't achieve wealth; we aren't free to take chances because we don't believe that our jobs will solve our future money goals. It took me a while to realize this.

I'm a regular guy with a family and modest education. I'm the classic son of immigrant parents who wasn't handed a golden spoon. I grew up in the lower middle class, in a loving family that taught me lessons in appreciating the value of a dollar. I was the only one in my family to graduate from university. Yet, I'd probably score lower on an IQ test than most.

The real difference between most others and myself is simple: I'm willing to take chances – calculated risks, to be fair. I love the world of investing. I consider choices from the "why" and "why not" perspectives just like other prudent people. I just don't over-think the "why not" for too long. If the "why not" isn't obvious, and many of the "why" reasons are, I react. I've seen many people miss opportunities by outsmarting themselves. I imagine you've heard of "paralysis by analysis"? That's exactly what this means. They miss their chance because they look for reasons why they shouldn't do something great. Ultimately, they'll convince themselves that it wasn't meant to be. It's such an awful way of looking at things. It's a way to excuse themselves from any accountability. I feel as though this is one stop away from the victim mentality. In the end, these people sit and complain about everything and end up no further ahead in life than they are today.

That's not you. That's not us. Not any more. That was who I was at one point, and it may have been you, too. That version of us is gone.

Early in my career, I decided to build a moat around my future, and nobody would take it from me. Once I had my plan for financial control, I could find true independence. I wouldn't allow myself to be trapped in a job with a paycheque. I just needed to figure out how to do that.

I had enough knowledge to know that investing was the way to achieve this goal. I started early, but remember that it's always better late than never. I just had to learn what to invest in. When I finally found that answer, my decision to follow that path brought me to where I am today, along with everything good in my life.

Your first goal is to use your salary to get enough cash to put to work through investing. The excitement lies in investing, not earning more from a job. A bonus or a pay raise is great, but only if you can turn that into more cash that you can invest.

WHY INVEST?

Stop me if this sounds familiar:

You went to school to get into the workforce with a high-paying job, which may or may not have happened. Maybe you bought your first place. It was entry-level, and it was fine. The mortgage was your first large debt, but you made it work. Next, you got a promotion and a pay raise. Congrats! Maybe you coupled up and found "the one." You needed more space and have a higher household income now, so you traded up. Sold the small home and bought a larger family home. You took on a larger mortgage. Another promotion! Maybe you will move again; maybe your family will expand. Maybe you hate your neighbour, or maybe you want a newer and larger home with a private office for your work-from-home space. During COVID, we needed to find ways to be happy at home, right? Along the journey, you've tacked on a new car or two and a gym membership. You bought the big screen TV and the upgraded laptop model.

As your pay level increased, so did your expenses. Mo' money, mo' problems. And so you're stuck in a world where you have to earn every week to pay your bills and keep the lifestyle that you now expect for yourself.

Are you investing? With whatever is left, sure. You've tossed some remaining money into a retirement account or an education fund for the kids.

I hate to tell you: you're living paycheque to paycheque. In Robert Kiyosaki's *Rich Dad, Poor Dad* world, he makes it very clear that you're in the Rat Race. You're running around in literal circles, never getting any further, never achieving more, and living beneath your potential. You are trading your time on earth for money.

Clearly, I'm painting a pretty dire picture, and of course, in no way am I suggesting you're stuck in this mud. I hope you're further ahead than the person described above! We've been misled and misguided over the years into believing that we'll be fine financially by doing what everyone else is. We won't – it's 100% crap. The way out is to make money work for you. The way out is to invest.

THE STORY THAT CHANGED MY LIFE

Back when I had that nine-to-five, I was just like everyone else. I was working on a tech team for a national insurance company. I had the same weekday routine: wake up early enough to shower, brush my teeth, get dressed and get ready for the day. I would take the same route to work every morning and follow the same pattern. I looked forward to little else than that first coffee at the office each morning. Perhaps you can relate.

My path took me past the same coffee shop on the way to the building elevator. I'd grab a coffee, smash that elevator button marked "14," and wait for the closing doors to reopen on my floor. When those doors did open, I would walk past a department on the way to my workstation.

When I looked to the right as I passed that department, I would always see the same gentleman working away on forms at his desk. I'd guess he was in his mid to late fifties and was overweight by a bunch. Once, when I paid more attention to his task, I saw that his job was filling in forms in triple-copy using old-school carbon copy paper. For those unfamiliar with carbon copy paper, it is a type of paper that has two or three plys. When you write hard enough on the top copy, it imprints several copies, so you can avoid filling in forms multiple times for multiple people. Nowadays, you'd scan or enter it digitally. In the mid-2000s, the technology did exist to handle this, but wasn't available yet at this company. His job didn't seem like one with great potential.

I would walk by this man daily on the way to the elevator. Until one day when I didn't.

It was a morning just like any other morning. I bought my coffee, rode the elevator, and got off on the same fourteenth floor. This time, though, things were different. There was nobody there when I got off. The entire department was gone. The man at the desk was not there, nor were any of his belongings on that desk.

The department had vanished. Downsized. Declared redundant, whatever – gone!

Instantly, I put myself in this man's shoes. What would I be thinking? I'd be thinking: I'm screwed. I would have lost all confidence. I would have quickly realized that my bright and joyous retirement had vanished. Nobody would want to hire me, being skillless, too old, and lacking interview skills. I may lose my family home. My wife is going to think I'm a loser. I'm a joke. This company that I probably gave my entire life and financial control to decided to stop being my lifeline, and it's too late to do anything about it. I'm sure it was all business, nothing personal.

I'd be absolutely panicked – maybe even suicidal at this point. Not having ever said a word to this guy, I somehow shouldered his entire burden, and I don't know why. It felt existential to me; it's difficult to explain. I still get choked up every time I bring up this story.

This experience hit me so hard that it may as well have happened to me directly. I'm thankful it didn't. I probably would have ended up just like him if it wasn't for that realization. I wouldn't have needed to make any meaningful change in my life. I'd have kept doing the same thing for years and years until my company told me they didn't need me around any longer. I knew that I needed to start investing as my way out.

WHAT IS INVESTING?

This is simple. Investing is when we delay using our own money. We give that money to someone else for that time and expect to be paid back with even more money later. I should be rewarded if I'm giving up my right to use my money. I expect to be rewarded for delaying today's gratification of using my money. At its core, investing is using money to make money.

WHAT CAN YOU INVEST IN?

Not all investments are created equal. There's a whole world out there built around giving people options or places to put their money. Some are very common, and others are a little more obscure. Here are some examples of common investment categories:

- Mutual funds
- Stocks
- Bonds
- Guaranteed investment certificates (GICs)
- Exchange-traded funds (ETFs)
- Cryptocurrencies
- Venture capital (VC) opportunities
- Small businesses
- Real estate

Have you invested in any of these? A lot of these are likely familiar to you. That's great! Most of these are available to regular people and are accessible to all. Sure, trading cryptocurrencies is entirely foreign to most people, and getting in on an exciting VC opportunity isn't likely an option for most regular folk. Think back to when Airbnb was looking for investment capital; nobody's likely to call us looking to raise funds for projects like these.

Most people will look at that list, find the option easiest to execute, and then make that their investment strategy. Someone they know knows someone else who made a lot of money in one of these categories. We don't want to miss that amazing opportunity, so we often follow the leader.

A lot of us end up in mutual funds – a pool of money from many investors is compiled and is used to acquire stocks of a number of companies, usually in a specific industry. Imagine a technology mutual fund. That fund would take bits of money from you and me and countless others and invest in companies like Amazon, Apple, Alphabet (Google's parent) and others. We don't want to go all in on one specific company. Mutual funds give us the ability to diversify a bit. Mutual funds have a fund manager that oversees the administration of all this. Mutual funds pay financial advisers for helping to bring more money into the fund.

Let's say fees for the manager and sales team come in at 3%, and the mutual fund you're invested in has a great year and achieves a 10% return. Of that 10%, 30% is paid in fees. If the fund makes 6%, the manager and sales team still take 3%. In this second case, you're giving up 50% of your return. How does that make you feel?

We take advice from a financial planner who directly benefits from the commissions of our investments in mutual funds. "Hey! Want to invest in these mutual funds with me?" We'll often blindly trust the adviser, just as my parents and I used to. It's our preference for the easy solution. To give these advisers credit, they do make it all sound effortless. We'll spend no time considering what we expect to earn from the investment because, well, *this is all stuff my adviser knows, and she knows more than I do, so just do it.* We're all guilty of following this strategy.

It's pressing the EASY button. You are not likely to find true wealth following this flawed strategy. I was reading Morgan Housel's *The Psychology of Money*. In it, he shares that 85% of mutual funds underperformed against the US stock market (S&P 500) in the decade leading up to 2019. Mutual funds can earn less than an alternative, which is a low-cost ETF. A common ETF could be an ETF that invests in the same stuff as the S&P 500. ETFs are becoming more popular because they don't necessarily have expensive sales networks or fund managers. Often, a computer algorithm performs the functions of a fund manager.

The infamous Warren Buffett follows this advice. In a 2017 interview, he gave investors this advice: "I think it's the thing that makes the most sense practically all of the time… [to] consistently buy an S&P 500 low-cost index fund." In 2021, he repeated his advice: "I recommend the S&P 500 index fund and have for a long, long time to people."

Buffett also has an ownership stake in a lot of real estate. For what that's worth.

Based on that report, when you are handing your savings over to a mutual fund to grow your money for you, 85% of the time the team does a worse job growing your money than if you invested your money yourself into an index fund or ETF. The mutual fund system is flawed (for investors). These funds must outperform the market to beat and cover these costs. It's not fair to the fund managers though they profit from the effort, and it isn't fair to us investors. This shocked me, and I will be liquidating my mutual funds when this book is published.

We're not going to do this any more. Not us. We're going to be

better than that. You see, most people will spend no time considering expected investment returns, looking at different asset
classes, understanding markets, understanding risk, or researching.
We'll turn a blind eye to the stuff we don't understand. And a
confused mind doesn't act. We're going to un-confuse ourselves,
starting right now. We've been duped into trusting the wrong
people all this time.

TAXES

I'm fascinated with taxes. In fact, I'm borderline obsessed with
taxes. More specifically, I'm obsessed with finding ways to reduce
how much tax I pay. I certainly pay my share of taxes, and I am not
suggesting tax evasion or avoidance as a viable strategy. However,
there are *so* many ways to reduce your tax liability legally and
ethically by making tax-efficient decisions.

We pay tax on our income as it is earned. Before we can spend
anything, we pay taxes. Then with what's left over, we pay tax on
all the goods and services we buy in the form of sales tax (HST or
GST). After paying, let's say, 50% of what I earn toward tax, I have
50% left. With that, I have to buy groceries and gas and pay my
utility bills. The 50% I'm left with is reduced further to cover 13%
HST on all the things I buy. I also have to pay property taxes on
the properties I own, and I have to pay land transfer taxes when
I acquire property. The car I bought and paid HST on is sold to
someone else that also has to pay HST (on the same car!). If she
resells it later, the buyer pays HST again. And so on and so on. More
HST was probably paid on the car than the car cost when it was
brand new – it's ridiculous! There are taxes everywhere.

I can justify the portion of taxes covering the services we need to function as a society. When it comes to applying tax for wealth distribution (because that's what it is), I'm not comfortable. When you finally realize that collecting and distributing taxes is a form of wealth distribution, I imagine you will feel the same. I want to preserve as much of my earned income as I can for my family, not for the government. Rant over. Sorry, not sorry.

If your goal is to maximize how much money is in your pockets after tax (and this *should* be your goal), you have to be mindful of *how* you're making money to pay less tax and keep more for yourself. There's no sense in paying more taxes than you need to.

In Canada, where I live, our government taxes you differently based on how you earn money. There are three main categories:

1. Ordinary income
2. Dividend income
3. Capital gains

You are taxed differently depending on which of these categories you're earning money in. When making "ordinary income," 100% of what you earn is subject to tax. What's in this category?

- Employment income, which is the largest category for most of us
- Interest income made on bank accounts, GICs
- Money lent out for interest

By far, most people earn money in this "ordinary income" category, which is taxable income to the government.

Dividend income is a bit more complicated. To earn a dividend, you have to be invested in an asset (usually a stock or a mutual fund) that pays the investor in a certain way, called a "dividend." It's just declared as such; it's a total tax thing. Money still moves from one place to another. The investor gets a tax break when money is earned in this particular category. It's complicated, though you'll end up with a tax break of just over 20%. The rest of the gain will be fully taxable.

The most tax-friendly way of making money is also considered the riskiest. It's called capital gains income. In simplest terms, you buy something low and sell it higher for a profit. The difference between the two numbers is the capital gain. In Canada, capital gains are 50% taxable right now.

I find it helpful to use an example with dollars to make this more relatable. For instance, if I'm having an amazing year and earn an additional $300,000 from three separate investments, I've made an additional $100,000 this year in each of the three categories. Assuming, for simplicity, I'm in a 50% marginal tax bracket, here are the results after tax:

1. Ordinary income: with this $100,000, I'll pay $50,000 in taxes and keep $50,000 in my pocket.
2. Dividend income: with this $100,000, I'll pay $30,000-40,000 in taxes and keep $60,000-70,000 in my pocket.
3. Capital gains: with this $100,000, I'll pay $25,000 in taxes and keep $75,000 in my pocket.

Moral of this story: I'd like to direct as much income as possible into capital gains, all things being equal.

Why are capital gains rates so much lower than ordinary income? It's simple, really, and it has everything to do with risk. Before you panic and put the book down at the sight of the word "risk," it's important to understand what risk means. Risk does not mean you will lose your money. Risk means the outcome of the investment is uncertain. It could lose value, OR it could go up – way up. Governments need to continue to encourage investment in companies and industries with uncertain outcomes because that's where innovation develops. We need people to take chances to better society as a whole. In exchange for your willingness to take a financial risk, your government gives you a break on your taxes to recognize that contribution. Seems like a fair trade to me. The investor wins, and society wins.

Now, if only an investment could create large returns on investment in the capital gains category without much risk. That would certainly be an investment that should be a top priority. The next chapter will focus squarely on this.

SCARCITY VS ABUNDANCE

I assume you are familiar with the concept of abundance versus scarcity. But just in case you aren't, I'll share how I understand these two words or mindsets.

Scarcity: there's not enough to go around, so I need to grab mine before someone else takes it from me.

Abundance: there is plenty for everyone. There are no limits on what I can accomplish because everything I need exists in large quantities.

Deep down, I think we all start life with a scarcity focus. Our first reaction when we're toddlers and someone takes our toy is to rip it back. We wouldn't have that reaction if we were predisposed to thinking in abundance. It's not our fault; it's just how we are naturally. That's okay because we can change.

Let me explain how economics and business work so you can see how scarcity and abundance theories are applied every day.

Let's look at a real estate brokerage. Realtors connected with a brokerage split their commissions with that office. There's no hard and fast rule, though they mostly all work on some commission-split arrangement. If a sale is 100%, the brokerage may collect 30%, and the agent keeps 70%. The 70/30 split isn't a rule; again, there are variations across the board depending on with whom you work. Sometimes, there's also an upper limit you can pay as an agent for a year, called a "cap."

In the first half of my real estate sales career, I worked for an office at Royal Lepage. While at my first office, I had a favourable commission split with a "cap." Back then, I paid somewhere around $15,000 of my earned commission fees to my office. As I matured, I found the office to be a bit stale and traditional. I wanted to grow, learn, earn more, and reach my true potential. Eventually, I started considering making the brokerage switch to where I currently hold my licence: Keller Williams Realty.

Keller Williams had a commission split, and they also had a cap. The only problem was that their cap was higher, and I would end up paying an additional $10,000 per year. You likely think what I thought – ouch!

In my scarcity mindset from back then, I couldn't get past the $10,000 I would *lose* each year if I moved to a more progressive and exciting brokerage. I knew that the new office would be able to help me grow and build a business and expand my reach. But, come on, $10,000 is a lot of money!

And so for years, I resisted switching to the better brokerage. My only consideration was that the move would cost me $10,000 (scarcity mindset). Luckily, I decided to stop thinking small and focus more on the $200,000+ of additional earned commissions I would expect from being a better Realtor for my clients. I did this by being around better agents, leveraging amazing tools and systems at Keller Williams, and taking advantage of the tremendous training and support at the office. I finally decided to think big, to see the abundance around me, and to shut up that little scarcity-focused monkey occupying my mind.

Looking back, had I started with that mindset when I first started transacting in real estate, I'd be on my own island now, sipping poolside cocktails served by my butler. I kid, of course.

I decided years ago to make decisions knowing that the world is abundant, not scarce. If we think with a scarcity mindset, we make some silly decisions. It's pretty dangerous, in fact, for many reasons.

Remember the toilet paper shortage at the onset of COVID? People thought (with a scarcity mindset) that we'd all run out of toilet paper. So people bought all the toilet paper that would fit in their minivans. They stuffed their garages with a never-ending supply of toilet paper so they could have all they needed until the end of time.

What good did that do? It created shortages for everyone else who *needed* another roll or two. It also raised prices for the people hoarding and for everyone else. In turn, the companies that produced toilet paper made higher profits. At the same time, everyone else drained their bank accounts to fund their purchases of toilet paper.

That's how a scarcity mindset can be influential. It's unnecessary for those not living near poverty levels, yet it's still the prevailing mindset in our society.

Scarcity clouds your judgment and doesn't allow you to make great decisions that are growth-based. Thinking small keeps you small.

Why do we even think this way? There's a fascinating section in *The Psychology of Money* where the author discusses how powerful the seduction of pessimism truly is. The point made in this book is how pessimism usually destroys optimism because there's more of it to go around and because it sounds smarter than optimism. It's referred to as "intellectually captivating." Pessimism receives way more attention than its nemesis: optimism. Optimistic humans often get put down for being naive and ignorant. By being optimistic, you aren't ignoring risk or being ignorant. It means that you feel good about an outcome. You know that not everything will be good all the time. Though you also expect things to work out most of the time.

In my experience, peers that hold optimistic outlooks outperform negative Nellies every time. They win in both earnings and happiness.

If we have to make an informed choice – and neither optimism nor pessimism will correctly predict the eventual outcome – why would you not choose to be optimistic? It will involve making changes to who you are, though it is possible. You can train your mind and change the way you think. That's why you are reading this book, and that's what you should set out to achieve right now.

SUMMARY

At the very start of this chapter, we discussed the two ways to develop wealth. You can work for it by trading your time (a job) or putting money to work for you (investing).

If you look around at the middle class, you'll notice the majority are doing the same thing, which is why the results are the same. Working a job more or less sets a ceiling on what you can achieve financially. If you make $100,000 in salary, you can certainly set a goal to earn $115,000 in the next year, and maybe you'll get there. Your job won't pay you $3,000,000, is the point. There's a fixed limit somewhere in your mind, your job, or both.

If you want to scale your growth, you will have to find a way to incorporate investing into your life. When you're on your way to becoming an active participant and not a spectator in your investing decisions and path, you're choosing to be intentional about growth.

Different investments will yield different results, which we now know. Taking that one step further, different assets will be taxed differently on their respective gains. This means you must be mindful of investing in categories you are passionate about and will net you more after taxes. That's the bottom line.

Nobody was born with a system of investments. It's up to each of us to see the world with an abundance mindset and not a scarcity mindset. We can control our thinking. When we think small, we'll be small. When you open your mind and realize that the world is loaded with abundance, you'll start to see possibilities for yourself that you missed before.

2

REAL ESTATE INVESTING

Ah, yes! Of course! Real estate to the rescue! Do you know why? Because *the house always wins*. This saying may have started in a casino, though it's true when considering real estate as an investment class.

First, let's eliminate the idea that this chapter – or book – is biased. I promise it's not. Yes, I'm a real estate broker and a real estate team leader. I will most certainly speak about how real estate investing is marvellous and how much it's done for me. Just because I am in the industry, it doesn't change my opinion (or the fact) that wealth-building through real estate simply rocks. I am so enamoured and obsessed with real estate investing that I've turned it into my job. Again, no bias here – I work in real estate BECAUSE I love the investing angle of real estate; it's not the other way around. Working in real estate has not given me rose-coloured glasses through which I view investments.

Now that I've got that off my chest, let's get into an exciting discussion about real estate investing, shall we? I have happily taken meeting requests from wonderful people who are dissatisfied with their past investment choices. We all thought we'd be "there" by now, yet many of us still live paycheque to paycheque. I mentioned this earlier, and I'll continue to draw awareness to this disturbing trend. It's because we're not living in the driver's seat – we're living in the passenger seat of our journey. Heaven forbid, what would happen if someone decided to take away your paycheque? Where would that leave you? You wouldn't be able to pay your mortgage or daycare fees, let alone keep up with the Joneses. You're probably approaching panic mode just imagining this.

If you don't want to worry about your financial future, your solution is probably to invest. With each paycheque, you're prudent, knowledgeable, intentional and savvy, so you put aside some of your earnings for a rainy day. You meet with a financial adviser (or not) and set aside some money. You believe that in ten years, or twenty years, or by retirement, you will be swimming in a sea of your own money. It'll be glorious.

Ten years later, you look at your balances in these investment accounts and think: well, I'm still young. I was told that the market goes up and goes down. It's normal. It's fine. We didn't make much money these ten years but gained some knowledge. We're wiser. We're better. At year twenty, you'll probably be saying the same thing you did during the first ten years if history is any indicator. You're certainly in better shape. You lived through some ups and downs again. It's still okay. However, you realize now that you aren't set up for the next twenty years if you stop earning and contributing. Uh oh. You've been putting money into this investment account for a while. You've been feeding the account. The account has not been feeding you. When you're finally at the point where you need money from a source outside of your job, you hope you'll withdraw a big lump sum of money. And when you sell or withdraw your investment, it'll be gone. It won't make you any more money. Game over.

If we don't continue to feed the investment, the investment doesn't work. We'll spend most of our adult life, our earning years, continuing to pour money into these investments, with the expectation that one day we can stop. One day, those investments will take care of us like we took care of them. When we stop putting money into those investments, we usually have to take money out of those same investments. And they'll devalue from that point on, forever, until all the money is gone. Of course, we'll have to hope this happens after we die.

This is not what an investment plan should look like. And so many of my real estate investor peers will tell you the same thing.

INVESTING 2.0 – REAL ESTATE EDITION

I want to shift gears and talk about a smarter kind of investment – one that is nothing like the horror movie I described above. I have no idea why this is a secret, but real estate is the greatest investment type. Deep down, I think we all kind of know this, though we never talk about it. More millionaires have been made through real estate than in any other way. I'm so confused that more people aren't engaged in this world. Commercial after commercial talks about financial planners and financial instruments, Registered Retirement Savings Plans (RRSPs) and Tax-Free Savings Accounts (TFSAs). And yet, the big bucks are absolutely in real estate investing for regular folks like us. And, no, they are not out of our reach.

You are likely a homeowner or grew up with a homeowner. At some point, you have noticed that real estate prices routinely increase. Even in a weak real estate market, do you expect real estate prices to be higher ten years from now? Would you expect prices to be higher five years from now? Everyone I've polled with that question has answered yes, regardless of the time measurement. Collectively, we don't feel that way about many asset classes. That's called consumer confidence. It's a market force that *wills* change. Enough of us believe in real estate that we effectively create that stability and growth in these assets. It's such a crazy and true concept.

If you want to learn why real estate investing is the much smarter alternative for an investor like you, keep reading. We're getting to that next.

THREE WAYS YOU MAKE MONEY IN REAL ESTATE

Let's learn about real estate investing and how real estate pays you in three ways. Go ahead, think of another investment that does that. When you own an investment property, you'll make money through:

1. Cash flow
2. Principal (mortgage) paydown
3. Appreciation of the property

I want to elaborate on each of these in isolation, analyze how they work after tax, and then we'll combine them.

1. Cash flow

Cash flow refers to the difference between revenues and expenses. Revenues, in this case, would be rental income, and expenses are all the things that must be paid to continue to own the property.

Typical expenses include mortgage payments, property taxes, maintenance and repairs, etc. When you subtract the two totals and end up with a positive number, you are "cash flowing." This is also called being cash flow positive. In most expensive markets, cash flow income is pretty awful. If you buy in these pricier areas, the best-case scenario is to start ownership with no cash flow (or even negative cash flow).

As you hold the property, the cash flow increases as rents increase. Over time, the investment usually gets better and better.

I live in Toronto. My city, admittedly, doesn't offer a lot of invest-ment properties that have amazing positive cash flow every month. Unless you're putting down a lot more than the minimum required to buy a property, you're not coming out ahead with hundreds or thousands each month in this category. Not right away, anyways. That cash flow will come in the future; it's just not great on day one. I'm fine to expect no cash flow (or even negative cash flow) when I buy property. I'm not concerned about category one at the beginning (categories two and three more than make up for the difference that's coming up).

Effect on taxes: money earned in this category is taxable at 100% because it's treated as ordinary income. You will face taxes annu-ally in this category if you are cash flow positive. If cash flow is negative, you may be able to reduce your tax liability.

2. Principal paydown

Each mortgage payment made is split into two parts: interest and principal paydown. When you have a mortgage, you are required to pay your lender interest for that loan. You're also paying some of your money toward reducing what you owe in the mortgage. Suppose you're working with a twenty-five-year amortized mortgage. In that case, if you kept the same mortgage terms for twenty-five years, all of your mortgage payments would eventually bring your mortgage to zero. In other words, you would have paid it off in twenty-five years.

When you're making your mortgage payment, you are guaranteed to pay down the mortgage. It is essentially creating equity for you. What is paid down is entirely your added equity. This guaranteed return is huge! The beauty of this section is in its simplicity. It doesn't matter if the market is up or down. As you collect rent and pay your mortgage, this will eventually get to zero if you want it to. When it does, those monthly rents don't need to be applied to a mortgage. They'll just live in your pocket.

Suppose you buy a place with a 20% down payment and secure a mortgage at 5% for twenty-five years (which is typical as of the time of writing). In that case, your return on your investment is 8.3% in the first year just by paying down your mortgage! And the return is higher every year than the one before it.

Again, with each mortgage payment you'll make, you are paying down the loan on the property. It's not even your money paying it down; it's all thanks to your tenants providing most or all the money to make those payments. If you do this long enough, the property will be paid off, and all of it by the tenants. You might have made the initial 20% down payment on the property, but the tenants will have paid the remaining 80% over the years, thank you very much. In exchange, you provided someone with a clean, safe place to live. Another win/win.

Effect on taxes: money earned in this category is taxable at 100% because it's considered ordinary income. Taxes are payable indirectly as you pay this down because the amount you pay toward the principal is not a tax deduction. I may have just confused you, but don't worry about it. Just know that taxes will be payable as you pay down what you owe to a small degree.

3. Appreciation

This is where home runs are hit, and anxiety is destroyed. Home prices do increase over the years. Property values rise far more predictably and consistently than stock markets. There may be dips, just as there are in every investment class. You won't see the 50% gains in a year that a stock market may make, and we certainly haven't come across the 50% drops in value that a stock market can have. The peaks and valleys are muted in real estate pricing. Through the years, nobody can deny that real estate appreciates.

Effect on taxes: Money earned in this category is taxable at 50% when you buy and hold because it is considered a capital gain.

COMMON WAYS TO INVEST IN REAL ESTATE

A common question I get from people new to investing is: "What should I buy?" All of the examples in this book follow a buy-and-hold strategy. Note that strategy matters more than the actual property you'll buy. It's more about you than it is about the investment itself. Buy-and-hold investments are passive in nature, and they don't require much time. Buy and improve strategies, in comparison, will take a lot of your attention away from other things in your life.

Though I recommend sticking with a buy-and-hold strategy, there are many different options for property types you can buy. We'll get into some of the major types of property investments below.

Single-family home

The most common type of property for first-timers is certainly a single-family home. This could be a condo, a detached house, or anything in between. The idea is that you would be renting to one person or one family.

It's not the most lucrative, though most people want to start the investing journey slowly and turn to this method for simplicity of understanding. It's okay; it's just hard to scale. If you have bigger goals, you'll run out of space for these in your portfolio quickly.

In a single-family home, you'll have less need for property management, and you may even build a relationship with the tenant. It's pretty personal, which can be a good and bad thing.

Pros:
There are low entry barriers, low cost, and the best mortgage rates.

Cons:
When a tenant leaves the property it is 100% vacant, and it becomes difficult to scale up.

Small multi-family home

A step up from a single-family home is a multi-family home. This single structure has two to four separate apartments in the building. Perhaps the building has been converted from a single-family home, or maybe it was purpose-built to be this way. A multi-unit home in a great area is always one of the best investments.

Pros:

You tend to get better insulation against the risk of non-paying tenants and vacancies, economies of scale (one roof to address, one insurance policy to pay for), and mortgage rates at low cost with big returns.

Cons:

There tend to be higher insurance costs and acquisition costs, and suites aren't always guaranteed to legally comply with building codes and zoning.

Pre-construction

As many flocked toward real estate investing, what was very common in Toronto was buying properties before they were built. Some people love this strategy, and others hate it.

There are a few different things to consider when buying a property that isn't built yet. Transaction costs involved in buying something on the resale market apply, as well as a slew of other costs specific to new construction.

Pros:

You get to pick all the finishes, the property often comes with a warranty, is highly desirable by tenants, and has a delayed deposit structure.

Cons:

There may be no rental income to offset investment for a while, much higher purchasing closing costs, and a lack of control over the schedule.

Buy and improve

Simply buying a property is work enough. When you decide to acquire real estate and do some work to it, you are in for a bit of pain, but hopefully, some added rewards.

There are many ways to search out options you intend to add value to by improving. Improving could be a renovation or a repair, or it may be converting the property's use from one type (commercial) to another (residential). As with all things in real estate, the sky is the limit.

I'm generally not a fan of introducing the complexity that a large-scale renovation would bring. At times, it may make sense for you, the investor, to consider this based on the post-conversion value.

I want to describe some popular options in the buy and improve space so that you're armed with the knowledge that makes you an educated investor.

Mangos Method

To be fair, this isn't the name this strategy is popularly known as. I called it Mangos Method because it was a strategy I created during a renovation I undertook. Novice that I was, I had no idea this was becoming my market's go-to strategy for real estate investment.

More commonly known as house-hacking or "BRRRRing," this method is employed when you: Buy, Renovate, Rent out, Refinance and Repeat. Hence, the BRRRR.

The best way to increase rents on an income-generating property (rents are your revenue, if you recall) is to have a property worth more on the rental market. All things being equal, a renovated home will rent for more money than a stale and dated home.

A house hacker would buy the stale home and start a renovation. The home is likely purchased with a short-term mortgage worth 80% of the value of the property. The goal would be to replace this mortgage shortly. When the renovation is completed, the property goes up for rent at a higher market value. With a newly renovated property and a tenant in place, the owner would apply for refinance – a replacement mortgage. The amount would come in at 80% of the value of the stunning and profitable home. The investor would pull out some or all of the equity used in the original purchase, plus the renovation, and use that money to start the process again.

When it works, it works amazingly well.

Pros:
Better cash flow and fast, forced appreciation.

Cons:
There's a risk of hitting a low market cycle and a risk of qualifying for a higher mortgage.

Flips
We've all seen people on TV buy homes for $50,000, spend $17,000 on them, and then sell them for $174,000. Flipping is such a trendy concept to watch and seems so easy!

Let me settle a debate, as someone who has front-row seats to these flips: that's never how they work. Those numbers are absurd. It's all fiction.

Flipping, in principle, sounds great. If you have access to construction crews that owe you a favour or are super handy, you have the advantage. For the regular person paying retail pricing for materials and labour to complete the renovation, it's a risky trade.

Delays always happen, caused by the availability of both trade and materials. Most people fund the purchase with a private mortgage (not a traditional bank) because they're easier to obtain and are more flexible on terms. That all comes at a high cost. So while you're building and waiting, you're paying a lot of monthly carrying costs.

In many places in Canada, the costs to buy and sell are so high that it takes away a lot of the profit you would have made. In Toronto, for example, if you bought a property for $1,000,000 and are hoping to renovate and sell for $1,300,000, you can expect to pay $150,000 just in closing costs. That's before even starting the renovation. Not only do you need to make money on the renovation, but you also need to cover all of these costs.

There could be great rewards, or this could bankrupt the investor.

This falls far outside of what I would consider, personally. It's far too active of an investment. I prefer the passive route, where I genuinely feel like there is little to no risk, especially if I have to ride out a negative market cycle.

Pros:
Quick cash when it works.

Cons:
There are many risks, as discussed, unpredictable results, and this method is very hands-on.

REAL ESTATE VS THE STOCK MARKET

Have a look at this chart. Let's compare the Toronto Stock Exchange S&P TSX Composite Index (aka: "the Canadian stock market") against home prices from the Toronto Real Estate Board since 1996. The slow-and-steady real estate investment closely matches the stock market trend, though without the anxiety of down years. I mean, look at the prices from 2006 to 2008. If you *had* to sell your stock or mutual funds in 2007 or 2008, you would have lost a ton of money. All the gains you would have made in the market from 2004 would have been wiped out. If you had to sell your real estate investment, though, you'd have been just fine at the time.

TSX Composite Index vs Toronto Home Prices

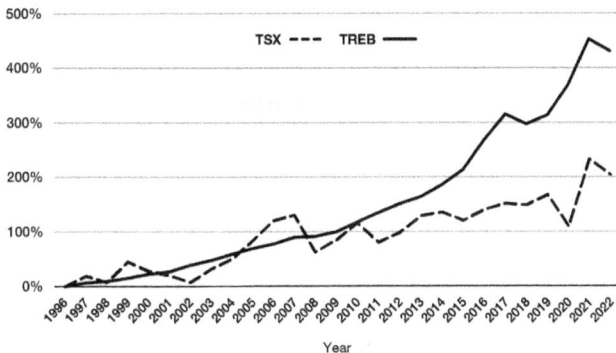

Year

Disclaimer: Some stocks will pay dividends, and that's not captured here. However, most of the stocks in the S&P TSX Composite Index do not pay dividends. Repairs to real estate will sometimes be required, and that will certainly take some added investment dollars. What is also not captured in this graph is that an owner can force appreciation through renovation, for example. Assessing all of that, the relevancy and accuracy of this graph are mostly unaffected.

LEVERAGE

If you're having a hard time getting through this chapter, hang on just a bit longer! I want to hit my very last point on why owning an investment property crushes the alternatives. I promise the reward is there if you stay with me a bit longer.

Quick: what's the first thing you think of when you hear the word "leverage"?

I know most of you see "debt" when you see that "L" word. Somehow, we've all been told to avoid debt and leverage. We're conditioned to this because we all read the same headlines.

....

"Canadians are over-leveraged!"
"Leverage is at an all-time high!"

....

It's time we faced the truth, though: **when used properly, leverage is a key to happiness**. Stick with me; I'll explain why and share my own experience with my favourite word: leverage.

Leverage doesn't mean debt. It *includes* debt, sure. It's just so much more than debt. I see leverage as this: sharing your responsibilities with others in exchange for your time and for your money. You could also phrase it as "offloading your responsibilities" if that helps you understand it. If you want more time and you're willing to pay for it, leverage lets you get away with NOT having to do what you don't want to. When you ask your neighbour to pick up your kids from school because you're running late, you're leveraging your relationship with your neighbour. When you pay someone to shovel your driveway so you can stay in and cuddle by the fire, you exchange your money to save some of your time. That's leverage. When you buy real estate and take out a mortgage for 80% of the value of that home, that's using leverage. This one is debt, sure. You're also asking someone to pay that 80% upfront (in exchange for monthly payments) so that you don't have to use your 80% right now.

Leverage. It comes in all kinds of forms.

Growing up as the son of immigrant parents who cared for nothing more than to pay down what they borrowed (mortgage), I learned early and often that debt (leverage) was bad. I believed this lesson so strongly that it probably set me back a few years in my financial evolution. We all likely have had that same programming installed in our minds.

My wife didn't grow up with gold bars in her family, either. One of her biggest fears growing up was not having money. She would hear "debt" and panic. She still does from time to time. The thought of owing someone money still gave her jitters until she saw how we used "good debt" to build a lot of wealth.

Now, my wife likes the idea of teaching financial literacy at home with our two young daughters. She's entrusted me with teaching this subject. I will teach the difference between good debt and bad debt. And I won't share the same lessons I learned from my lovely parents; I can tell you that.

Why do we think debt is so bad? Or that all debt is bad debt? When you owe a friend some money, you should pay them back in full immediately. However, is that debt still bad if you're borrowing money and that money is making you more money than it costs you? Is leverage the worst thing in that scenario? Everything changed for me when I shifted my perspective on using "other people's money" (OPM) to make more money for myself. OPM opens the door to making a lot of money.

I'll quickly share how this works using an example. Using the previous scenario again, if I borrow money to buy a property, I generally borrow 80% of the value at, say, 5% interest (this is the mortgage). When the property appreciates (not IF, but WHEN) – call it 3% in my first year of ownership – it appreciates 3% on 100% of its value, not on the 20% I've invested. The 3% gain on the home's full price translates to 15% (3% x 5) because my investment was ⅕ of the value of the home. If this happened in a year, I would have earned 15%, and it would have cost me 5% to borrow that money to make that money. I traded 5% for 15% using leverage. See what I mean? I've simplified it, but you get the point.

At this stage in my life, leverage has added meaning. Leverage means way more than debt or "OPM." Leverage of time is now the single most influential factor in my life.

We've heard this often: time is the one thing you can't make or buy more of. It just doesn't work like that. Time is our most precious commodity.

So I've consciously decided to use leverage to keep my time to myself. I want to do the things that I want to do. I can apply my financial gains to the most important things: family and freedom. I could do everything independently and give up my time in exchange for earnings. It's how I started my career and built a business worth having. It was what I needed to do; it was what I wanted to do. I still very much love to work.

I have realized quite clearly that I have to be selective about what I do with my time. Even if it means choosing to be a couch potato and channel surfing, that's time I could be spending working or doing other things. When I replaced my salary with real estate, I introduced these as choices I could freely make.

When I choose not to do something – to trust others to do it for me (often in exchange for money) – I'm using leverage to retain my time. It's a tough pill to swallow. And don't tell my parents, who would write me off if they knew I chose not to earn more when I could so that I could watch Netflix and relax.

Leverage gives me time with my girls, lets me watch the Raptors game, and allows me to have a date night with my wife while clients submit offers. Leverage allows me to vacation – or work from away – for months at a time. I have a team of people in place to ensure all of my promises and obligations are looked after (probably even better than I could do).

Leverage has allowed me to help the next generation of earners on my real estate team stand on their own two feet, buy their own homes and exceed in their careers. Leverage has created better Realtors on my team than I ever hoped. I allow my team to learn and expose them to a lot; now, they are better than I am at everything!

Leverage made all of this possible.

LEVERAGE IN REAL ESTATE

When you buy a stock, you're paying the full price of that stock. If it's a $1,000 stock, you pay $1,000. With real estate, you're typically only going to need to fund 20% (NOT 100%) of the property's value. However, the appreciation of the property happens at 100% of its value. For every 1% the property appreciates, your return on your investment is 5%. If property prices go up 5%, you're up 25% return on your investment. Isn't that crazy? That, my friends, is the power of leverage. One can also access leverage in stock investing through margin accounts. It's a similar concept, though with far more restrictions and limitations. There's a reason why lenders are much more comfortable lending up to 80% of the value of real estate indefinitely, and not so with stock investors. The risk/reward paradigm favours real estate.

I believe in the power of repetition. I will repeat certain points in this book to make sure the messaging really hits home.

Remember the chart comparing Toronto real estate prices to the stock market? Let's look at that again, but now let's wonder what it would look like if we're making all of that appreciation based on 100% of the home price and knowing that we're only putting down 20% to buy it. Now, look at that chart again (you have permission to say, "Wow").

Taking all of this in, what if we could execute a strategy just as described? A never-ending cash flow stream that will continue to pay every month and does nothing to devalue the actual investment. We don't need to worry from month to month about continuing to fund our investment with a paycheque if the rents cover the cost of ownership. We're paying down the mortgage

TSX Composite Index vs Toronto Home Prices (with leverage)

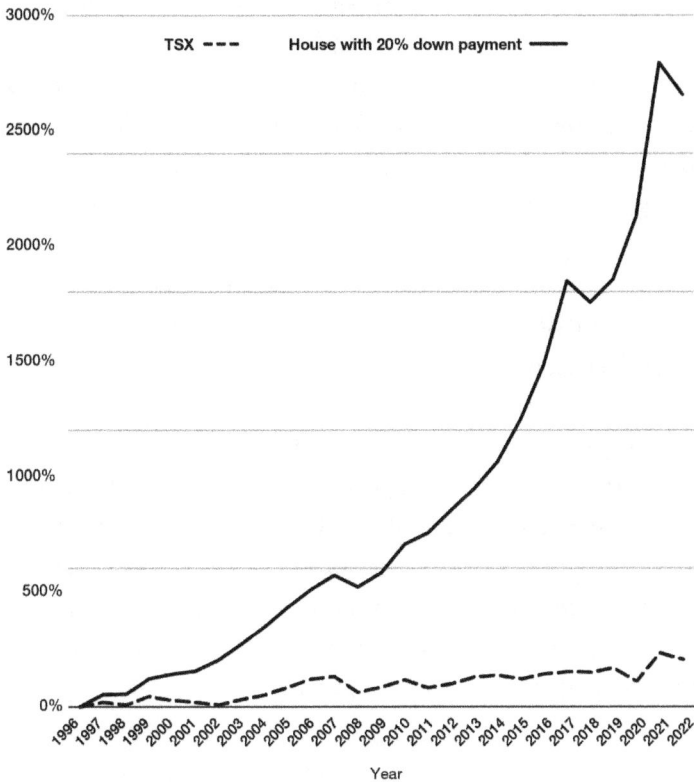

without any of our own money. The investment keeps growing and growing in value, and the appreciation is amplified because of the way we used leverage. Can you do all of this with stocks and mutual funds? Nope.

I do feel that many of us know better than to only consider traditional investment options. I think a lot of us believe mutual funds or stocks are our only investment options because the cost to play in that game is so low. I'd say that pretty much all of us consider this the only accessible investment available to us. I used to think that, but now I know better, and I'll never go back to only considering those inferior options. It's real estate only for me.

You probably knew all of this in the back of your mind, but you couldn't connect the dots. All of the wealthiest people own lots of property. Now that you've seen this and realized the truth, what will you do with this knowledge?

The further I dive into real estate and personal finance, the more I discover that most people *avoid* investing in real estate. The question I keep asking myself is: Why?

I'm living, breathing, and walking proof that investing in real estate – even in small doses – can positively impact financial freedom and independence. It can reshape you and the people around you and position you all for an amazing future. When asked, I happily share what this focus has been able to provide for my family. Yet, I still see reluctance from many people in my world when it comes to executing their real estate investment plans.

In Canada, specifically, real estate has had amazing and consistent success. This growing nation takes on more net residents each year. It's a safe and inclusive country, with health care and education for all, and where there are societal rules. When I analyze supply and demand, it's clear that prices in Canadian real estate will continue to rise in many more robust markets. There is no dispute that this is true for the long term.

So why isn't everyone who can invest in income properties in Canada choosing to do so?

I'm fortunate to speak with people exactly in this position. More often than not, here's why people don't add real estate to their investment portfolio: they don't want to be landlords. It's not so much about affordability; it's about lifestyle. They're investing elsewhere, and they have the money somewhere. But the fear of being a landlord is crippling.

They expect that being a real estate investor means agreeing to become a landlord. I think the *landlord* title somehow translates into a *slumlord* in the mind of the non-investor. And, of course, nobody wants to be regarded as one of those people. Ew, gross.

Most people ignore the billion (or so) benefits of investing in real estate. They won't consider for a moment what the benefits of such an investment are for themselves and their family, like the tax breaks, the passive income and the financial control. And they can't get past thinking of themselves as a (*bleh*) landlord.

I know too many wonderful people who are misinformed and misguided. You don't want to be a landlord? You don't have to be. Property management companies everywhere will happily be the landlord for you. At the same time, you can remain the investor. We'll go over this in part two when we discuss the Replace Method. I'm on a mission to stop these people from throwing away their chance for a better life with greater financial rewards all because *they don't want to be landlords.*

Assume you can outsource the "burden" of being a landlord while retaining all the good that comes with owning property. With the awareness that massive wealth will build, will you still choose to miss your chance to claim these rewards?

My team's investing plan for clients shows how we expect to

double their investment dollars in under five years with minimal risk. Up to this point, we've done it in less than five years (and sometimes under a year!). It can be done without you ever having to claim the landlord title you've been avoiding. This is how you'll progress toward an eventual replacement of salary income.

By reading this book, you're educating yourself on proven investment strategies that balance risk and reward far better than the well-known literature.

The question you have to ask yourself is this: if you had a chance to invest in real estate, knowing what you know now, would you?

TUAN'S INSIGHTS:

One of the most influential people I've met is a good friend named Tuan Tran. Tuan's a colleague in my office; he's been a top Realtor forever, and he's just a great human being. He recently shared this nugget about why he is a real estate investor. He unapologetically insists he's lazy by nature. And it's because of that laziness that he chooses to invest in real estate. You might be wondering, how does this make sense? Here's his rationale: "Real estate isn't easy to sell; I can't press 'sell' on a screen and liquidate the asset. If I could, I would. Real estate takes effort to sell, so I won't do it because laziness wins. Delaying selling has made me a fortune."

He may be lazy, but he knows what real estate has done for him and his family. Good on you, Tuan. You're my hero!

Let's jump back to our discussion about taxes to refresh our knowledge of real estate taxation.

Money earned in appreciation is tax-preferred because capital gains are 50% taxable in Canada. One half of the gain will not be taxed, while the other will be. Nearly everything else, including ordinary income, is taxable at 100%. Every dollar would be taxable, which means you'll keep less when the dust settles.

For example, suppose you're in the 50% tax bracket and are earning an extra $30,000 in a particular year from a bonus or a regular interest-paying investment. In that case, you'll pay $15,000 in tax and keep $15,000 for yourself. If you make that same amount via the appreciation of an income property and sell the property that year, you'll pay half of that tax ($7,500) and get to keep $22,500. After-tax returns should be the ones given the most attention if you're looking for the best results. Intention matters!

Returns on appreciation are truly amplified in a growing market when using leverage. When you buy real estate, you invest 20% of the down payment and borrow the rest, and your rewards are based on 100% of the price when it appreciates. You can share the purchase dollars with a lender (your 20% vs their 80%), though you don't need to share the gains. Those are 100% yours. For every 1% the market increases, you see 5x, or 5% in this case!

SUMMARY

Investors generally love real estate as their investment of choice. The security and stability, coupled with the great returns and the multiple ways to experience growth, make this the world's greatest investment – especially when considering risk versus return.

Real estate makes you money in three ways:

1. Cash flow
2. Principal (mortgage) pay down
3. Appreciation

Eight billion people populate the world. All of us need places to live. Residential housing stock will never go out of style. Real estate is still very much tangible and essential in a digital world. Sure, there may be some market shifts, but you can rest assured knowing that these shifts will be far less extreme than our stock or crypto investor peers are experiencing at the same time.

The straight buy-and-hold strategy of investing in real estate is always a winner because real estate appreciates very handsomely. Returns on appreciation are truly amplified in a growing market when using leverage.

Even in down markets, real estate always provides a return when you're buying the right place. There's no real estate problem that time can't fix. The house *always* wins.

PART TWO:

THE REPLACE METHOD

3

STEP 1: REFLECT

When was the last time you actually looked in the mirror? Not to check your hair or to spot the blemish. When did you last take a deep look at yourself, into yourself, to seek to understand? Probably never, right? I went years without looking in a mirror. Life's too busy, and it's full of distractions. Who has the time or can be bothered to make the effort?

We live with blinders on, intentionally or unintentionally. We get through days. We're told to show up at work every Monday at 9 a.m., save our money, buy into benefits, and invest money in our RRSPs. If you don't know what an RRSP or a RESP is, don't worry. I will explain these concepts in this chapter.

Let's get introspective for a second. Take a moment to ask yourself the following questions:

- Are you where you thought you'd be right now?
- When was the last time you looked at your investment statements?
- How often are you saving? How much are you saving?
- Do you understand what an RRSP is?

- Are you on track to hit your goals?
- If you lost your job, how long could you survive?
- How much money do you have saved?
- What are your account balances in your savings and investment accounts? Is that enough?
- How many more years do you need to work until you reach the stage where you have enough?
- What do you love to do, and how can you make more time for that?
- Is each day starting to feel the same as the one before?

The false security of a salary permits us to ignore these questions. Recently, I came across a quote that stole the thesis of my thoughts, "Your salary is the bribe they give you to forget your dream." Though I paraphrase, this idea was made popular by Segun Awosanya, known as Segalink, a Nigerian Realtor, human rights activist and business consultant. I think it's such a perfect way of describing what happens to most of us. The nine-to-five lifestyle can be a trap. Even if you love your job, it probably prevents you from doing other things you love. Plus, you are likely dependent on the job financially to live your life.

If you've ever thought about retiring, even if for a second, you'll have thought about this RRSP thing that our governments and banks offer. They would have us believe this is the solution to our money problems as we get older. Most of us think they're right! But the joke is on us.

If you've been convinced to contribute to your kid's Canadian RESP, you've been duped.

REGISTERED ACCOUNTS (RRSP AND RESP)

The RRSP and RESP solutions we have been pitched are all bark and no bite. You've got to take a detailed look at these two account types to understand. I'll try to keep this conspiracy-theory free.

Our government wants us to save so that we aren't a burden in our old age. They want us to be able to send our kids to university so that we can have an educated workforce in the future. They want us to fund these life stages on our own, so they entice us to do that by offering a few nuggets in exchange. If you set up these types of accounts, they give you some benefits. These accounts are registered with the Canada Revenue Agency (CRA).

We comply because the masses agree with RRSP and RESP savings, and the marketing reinforces the message. We see commercial after commercial and poster after poster, all telling us the same thing: this is what we should be doing with our money. At some point, we've all been sold to and forced to believe it.

And because it is so easy to open one of these accounts and start investing right away, we'll choose the easy option every time. We outsmart ourselves, we outsource the understanding.

YOUR RRSP

Do you know why retirement savings plans exist? Here's a brief history of the subject:

Income taxes were a new concept in 1917, and were created as a way for the Canadian government to help pay for all the funds needed during the First World War. It was meant to be a temporary tax to help finance the war. Over a hundred years later, income taxes still exist and continue to increase in percentages of income. Slowly and surely, we must pay more and more of what we earn to help finance the government.

The government designed registered retirement plans as an incentive that offered us an *exception* to income taxation. It was a "Hey, we're taking care of our people!" type of publicity stunt they put on. Our governments created a plan to tax us on our incomes, and now they throw us a bone to create an exception to their own rules. That doesn't sit right with me.

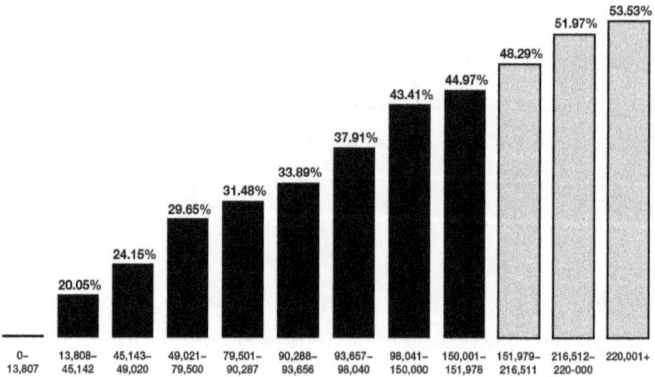

Source: mdtax.ca

Enter the RRSP, or Registered Retirement Savings Plan. To fully understand how the RRSP works, one must fully understand the tax bracket architecture of our economy. The numbers have changed over time and will change in the future. It doesn't matter what the exact rates are; knowing how these brackets affect you is most important. Canada's tax system is a "progressive" or "graduated" tax system.

For the first portion of your income, you pay the government a percentage of that income through income taxes. When your income exceeds that limit, you are graduated to the next tier, where the tax rate is a bit higher. Keep earning, and you reach the limit on that bracket, and you're into the next one with even higher tax rates. The one after that is even higher, and so it goes on. The tax percentages increase until you hit the top tax bracket (if you're fortunate enough) in this graduated system. As of 2022, the top tax bracket is reached when income is around $220,000 annually. Once you hit that figure, every dollar you earn above is charged tax at the highest possible rate. In that case, the income tax on that extra dollar is just over 50%. Call it a reward for being a top earner.

Again, suppose you're fortunate enough to be a top earner. In that case, you're rewarded by exposing your top dollars to the highest possible rate. This has discouraged friends of mine from earning in the past. Their logic leads them to see this as working for half of their earnings, a scarcity mindset working at full speed. This hurts our economy's output.

Getting back to the RRSP, the benefit they are giving us is a tax deferral opportunity. If you put money into this RRSP, you get to reduce the income you report in that year by the same amount of money you contributed. In lowering the income you report on paper, you reduce how much taxes you'll pay that year.

Let's work through a simplified example – suppose Jane had a great year. She earned a whopping $250,000 in income! Congratulations, Jane! The amount Jane earned toward the end of the year went from $220,000 to $250,000 because of a performance bonus. That extra $30,000 could do wonders for Jane's family. Instead, with

Jane being in the highest marginal tax bracket, Jane will have to share roughly $15,000 with the government in the form of income tax. Jane walks away with just $15,000 of that $30,000 she earned. But if Jane decided to deposit that $30,000 bonus into her RRSP, she would lock up her savings in exchange for a lower reported income on her tax return. She'll report $220,000 as her annual income, and Jane won't get to use her bonus money for a long while. Later in life, Jane and her government presume she will have lower earnings as she ages and enters retirement. At that point, Jane could slowly withdraw her RRSP savings; however, she'll be charged income tax because that withdrawal is considered income. Though, for Jane's sake, the hope is that she's earning far less in retirement and paying taxes at a much lower marginal rate at that time. In a nutshell, the RRSP is a vehicle for tax deferral.

THE FLIP SIDE OF THE RRSP

I truly believe our government uses tax deferral as a bribe. We are coached into planning to earn less as we age past a certain point. They expect that we will earn less in the future. What if you don't earn less? What if you want to earn more in your sixties and seventies than you're earning now? What if you expect your future to be brighter than your past or your present? Deferring taxes by locking them up in this bank account prison actually works *against* you. Nobody seems to realize or publicize this concept.

I understand that the government is trying to save the nation and us from dependence on government funding and social security. The truth is that people, for the most part, do not save. Most people will live paycheque to paycheque for a long time. I genuinely hope this is not your current strategy after reading this chapter. If it is, I hope you find the courage to face these facts and recognize that this is a losing strategy.

Banks with mega marketing budgets also want us to fund our RRSPs because a dollar deposited in their account does a lot of good for them. They get to multiply that dollar into more dollars, and they'll lend out and charge interest for far more than they are paying you for holding your money. They pay you 0.3% interest to hold your money, but they lend it out at 4% and keep the difference. Next, they'll encourage you to invest in their mutual funds. Mutual funds provide excellent wealth for their fund managers, their operations and, most importantly, their company's investors.

Banks do an excellent job of convincing us to open our RRSP and start investing with them today. We, in turn, do a great job of believing them. That big chart on their wall sure is inspiring. They are right; you would be rich today if you invested $100 in the stock market in 1884. They market very well to us, and they control the messaging.

If your account balance in your RRSP at retirement was $200,000, would that be a lot of money? How about $400,000? $500,000? It seems like it may be a lot of money at first glance.

Imagine you are sixty-five, and you've hit retirement age. Amazing! Let's also imagine you will be healthy, vibrant and excited. You're going to live to ninety. You'll travel, and you'll buy that sports car. You may have a plus one with you. A year of spending may take $100,000 of today's dollars. How many years will you live off that $200,000 or $500,000 in your RRSP? Don't forget that money will still be taxed in the future. $500,000 is NOT $500,000. You want to do a bit of travelling. Maybe buy a boat.

You spend $100,000 in your first year of retirement. Then you realize the money won't go as far as you imagined it would. Is there a danger of you not having enough money to live on? Does that future excite you any more?

I hope you're scared out of your mind right now. You should be. In all likelihood, you are not prepared for a great retirement. If you like horror stories, start surfing the web to learn about the Canada Pension Plan and how it's quietly running out of money. Increasing income taxes on the rest of us will be the only way to keep the beast afloat. Social security should not be your default retirement fund. It doesn't look like it'll be able to survive much longer.

JOE'S STORY

RRSPs don't always follow your life's plan. I want to share a true story of what happened to someone close to me who followed mainstream advice from a typical financial planner.

One of my all-time favourite people on Earth is Joe. My wife and I admire him greatly. He is a great father to two wonderful and productive people, and a loving grandfather and husband. In the early 90s, Joe left Europe for a better life in Toronto as a single father. Hard work and focus brought him everything, and he lives the Canadian dream.

After a morning swim at the YMCA and a shot of espresso, he mounts his bicycle (or sometimes motorcycle) in skin-tight span-dex, bright yellow shoes, and the trendiest eyeglasses and hits the road. Joe, in his sixties, bikes to work if it isn't raining. I'd guess it's about twenty kilometres each way, and much of that is uphill. He is undoubtedly the healthiest person I know.

He leaves his wife every day to trek to the office where he's a software engineer. They head south on vacation yearly, chasing warm seas to scuba dive and enjoy the good life. Once Joe retires, the plan is to travel, see more of the world, and be active and explore. Scuba is calling! Europe is calling!

How will Joe retire? Of course, with the money he's been preserving in his RRSP! Joe is approaching $1,000,000 in assets in that account. Forty years of compounded savings will eventually reach a considerable number. That and selling their family home will allow Joe and his wife to buy a small condo in the city and have a healthy budget to do everything they've dreamed of.

But during COVID, things changed. Joe got sick, unfortunately. Life had plans that didn't align with Joe's. The sickness defeated Joe and left his wife a widow. Their retirement plans will never be realized.

Even the best of us can't tell when our time is up.

As Joe neared the end, he was aware enough of his health to know that he'd never spend three months in Tulum sunbathing and scuba diving. He wouldn't get his chance to sip espresso daily on a patio in an exotic location. These realizations couldn't have been easy to acknowledge or accept.

To the best of my knowledge, for over twenty years, Joe followed the advice of a financial planner that indeed suggested RRSP saving as a way to minimize taxes. As we covered earlier, when contributing to retirement savings in an RRSP, you effectively reduce your taxes payable *today*. The logic is rooted in the expectation that you'll earn less money when you retire, so your tax bracket and tax dollars will be lower. We live expecting to earn less as we enter our golden years. Joe did; he must have. Otherwise, why contribute this way?

A few months before Joe passed away, he was made aware that when people die, our estate is required to settle our affairs, and tax liability is due. Everything we own is deemed sold (including our RRSPs), and it's all taxable. In his final tax return, Joe's estate had to declare $1,000,000 of RRSP savings as income, along with his work earnings when he was healthy earlier that year. Those earnings plus the RRSP savings that had to be withdrawn upon death were all included as "regular income" to the government that year. That pushed almost all of Joe's earnings into the absolute highest tax bracket. The government doesn't have feelings and doesn't care about what this means to Joe or his family. The government ensures everything is deemed sold or liquidated. Then they take all of that into a generic "income" category, which the deceased now has to declare as income in a single year's return. Joe's children from a previous marriage were listed as beneficiaries on that RRSP, so there was no transfer to Joe's wife's RRSP. His wife and children had to write a cheque to cover Joe's tax liability of around $500,000 shortly after his death.

Poof – $500,000 gone.

The worst part was that Joe realized this a few short months before he passed. Despite all of his efforts, everything he had worked toward, saved toward, and planned for was going to taxes. He delayed using his hard-earned money while he was healthy and youthful in anticipation of a great retirement. Life, again, had other plans.

The RRSP cost Joe's family money and brought worry into his final thoughts.

This true story angers me every time I think about it, and it should anger you. We can't change what Joe's RRSP achieved (or didn't achieve) for Joe. We can change how we view government retirement savings plans and learn to trust ourselves and not our governments to look after our families and us.

YOUR RESP

If you are a parent and feel compelled to help your kid with university costs when they're ready, you are amazing and should be thanked. So, thank you.

I'm not sure where I first heard about the RESP. Once you learn about it, you almost feel as though you've been let in on this wonderful secret. It's loaded with the promise of free money! Yay!

The logic behind a government push toward education savings is noble. They need to nudge us to help fund tomorrow's leaders without the need for these future students to incur crippling and inescapable debt from the costs of acquiring their education. Thankfully, education costs in Canada are still significantly below those in the United States. It doesn't nullify the burden, but it's just a little more accessible overall.

Suppose a parent or grandparent is incentivized to spend some savings on a child's future education. In that case, we are taking steps as a society to secure our future leaders and doctors, for example. People in our communities need to be educated. Taking away that opportunity from a potential student is devastating for all. The government needs to and does prioritize an educated population and workforce. The government's primary tool to encourage education savings and planning is the RESP.

The RESP's winning feature is its contribution-matching component. For the first $2,500 contributed to a child's RESP each year, Canada matches 20% (up to $500) of that contribution directly in the RESP. Another great benefit is that the money that grows in the RESP (if the money grows) does so tax-free to the child.

Sounds great, right?

THE FLIP SIDE OF THE RESP

It does sound great until you drill down a bit deeper. What happens if your child doesn't go to a qualifying post-secondary institution? Life happens. Death happens. You can transfer the money to a sibling if there is one. If you need to cash out and take this money back, you'll lose all of that "free money" in that deal, *and* getting your money back in your wallet is tricky.

Imagine if you're fifteen years deep into this plan when bad luck makes it impossible for your only child to get to university. All these years of saving and building you thought you were doing are wiped out. That can't be a nice feeling.

If you've not sat down and done your own math on how much is needed to go to university for four years in Canada (tuition, room and board), it's time you did. We'll work through an example here that won't be specific to your family if you have kids. However, it will undoubtedly demonstrate the point.

First, let's make some assumptions. Tuition costs in Canada are coming in at around $7,000 per year for 2022. At our current high inflation rate, books, rent and meals would cost about $22,000 for one year if your child went to university in 2022.[1] That number will only increase over the coming years. Eighteen years from now, when this mythical child heads to university in 2040, that four-year program, room and board will cost $135,000.

What are your RESPs on track to be when your child hits eighteen? Have a look at your statements. Put this book down, look up your numbers, and return to this chapter.

Suppose you realized your "astonishing returns" in your RESP point to an account value of $35,000. It's time to rethink your strategy of relying on your RESP to pay for university.

It's not your fault; it's not their fault; it is what it is. Forcing parents to save for university is a truly noble plan. Something is better than nothing, hands down.

At the same time, shame on the banks and the marketers for making us believe that this RESP was a set-it-and-forget-it plan. Parents are often coached into thinking that the money issues

---

1 https://knowledgefirstfinancial.ca/how-much-to-save-for-education/

they're sure to face for those university years are solved when they go the RESP route. Every single parent I've spoken to while researching this book confirmed that they are not on track to be fully financed by the time tuition comes due.

CURRENT ISSUES: A NOTE ABOUT INFLATION

Inflation is a topic that continues to be ever-present. I won't go too deep into politics or fiscal policy on this. Suffice it to say you can expect inflation to rise for the foreseeable future.

In periods of high inflation, hard assets are the ones that generally retain their value the most. Hard assets are tangible assets or things that you can touch and feel. Bars of gold, for example, are hard assets. So are houses.

If nothing else, history has proven that real estate rises with inflation. Suppose you are sitting on money in the bank during periods of high inflation. That money is losing value with time. Still, if you use that money to acquire assets during inflation, those assets increase in price because of inflation. Choose wisely.

Some people prefer to view real estate as risky during down markets or recessions. My question is: do we think company stocks won't lose more value than housing during a recession? I do not have the research to back this up. However, I feel much more comfortable in a recession holding a home as an investment over stock in a company that may or may not continue to exist. That home will outlast the recession. Real estate has proven to increase in value in Canada. If we're in a recession, I feel more confident investing in real estate than all other asset classes.

RESP OR A NEW CONDO PURCHASE

Right around when my first daughter, Mia, was born, I heard about the RESP. I shared the great news with my wife. We called a planner and got an account set up immediately, and we begged them to take our money so we could apply for the "free money." Everyone called it the no-brainer strategy.

In eighteen years, we'd be ready financially for Mia to head to university. The total investment needed was $2,500 yearly for eighteen years. This would total $45,000.

At about the same time, there was an emerging market in my real estate world toward new condo construction in my growing city. I was excited about the prospects of buying this type of real estate.

My wife and I made another decision at that time to buy a small condo as part of this project. We investigated the area, the pricing, and the plans. Overall, we felt terrific about the potential this investment would provide. We helped a few others acquire their condos in this complex as well. It just made sense for those of us who decided to buy.

The condo we bought cost $300,000. Buying a condo before it was built broke the deposit structure into several smaller deposits spread out over a year. Ultimately, we needed to put up $60,000 in total across a year to acquire our condo. Thankfully, we could afford this and were keen on growing our wealth.

It took a few years to complete the building, and when it was, we had it rented pretty quickly. We were careful and found a glorious tenant. We agreed on a rental contract at the lower end of the rental market value, and we never really increased her rent. She took amazing care of the place and never really called us for any issues, so we wanted to reward that by not increasing her costs. We were probably out of pocket $100-200 each month because our rent didn't entirely cover the costs associated with ownership. Even though we were not making great cash flow, we were paying down the mortgage we owed more than the $100-200 we contributed out of our pockets. Most of our mortgage payments came from our tenant during her three years there (it was under construction for the other four years). At the same time, the place was appreciating in value. It was a trade we knew we were getting into, and it really was a win-win scenario in this case.

Fast-forward to seven years after we first put pen to paper to buy that condo. The condo had appreciated from $300,000 to $520,000, and we had paid down $20,000 in our mortgage there. When you add that up, that's $240,000 of equity created. Our $60,000 investment had just returned $300,000. That's a $240,000 gain, or 400% return on investment in those seven years.

If we were paying $150 per month for a property manager in addition to those three years, that would take away $5,400 from our overall return. Basically, negligible.

Astonishing results, right? Don't get me wrong; luck may have played a role. The timing worked out for us. I wouldn't ever expect results like these on a purchase. These numbers are large and may be difficult to duplicate today. Not impossible, however, and I'd like to leave you with that point. There are always great options out there. If our results had underperformed these, it would still have been the best thing we could have done.

This is a great time to check on how that RESP is doing. After seven years of maximizing our contributions ($17,500) through mutual fund investment and applying for government grants, our total RESP savings came in at a whopping $27,000. We had a 54% return on investment over the seven years, including the 20% bump from the government's free money. At this pace, with our RESP, we wouldn't have enough money to fund our daughter's education. We were at $27,000 of $135,000 and nearing the halfway mark.

The condo, at seven years of ownership, could cover both my children's costs if we stopped right there and left the money in a safe savings account for the next eleven years. Take that, RESP.

YOUR CURRENT REAL ESTATE INVESTMENTS

If you're already a real estate investor, you've no doubt realized the awesomeness of your investment decisions. When you compare the equity you've created in this category against your mutual funds, I'm willing to bet your real estate has outperformed. You can move to Step 2 in this book if this is the case.

To the ones who remain, there's an answer to these retirement and education problems above. That answer is simple: acquire your first income property.

Remember the three ways you make money with real estate, and apply them to your life. Let's work through it together. When you acquire your first income property, you're not likely to make much money each month in terms of cash flow. That will come in the years that follow. When your tenant starts paying your mortgage principal, you will start making money immediately. In a slowly appreciating market, you can expect to turn your $50,000 equity investment into $100,000 in less than five years, or $100,000 into $200,000 during that time, and quite safely.

SUMMARY

You don't need to be focused on retirement or education. Although this chapter focused on these issues, the point is that it's super important to know what you want, plan to get that, and start making changes if you realize you're off the path.

Simple truth bomb, my friends: if you keep doing what you're doing, you'll keep getting what you're getting. If you repeat your behaviour today, tomorrow will look identical to today. These don't seem like scary words, though they should read like a gut punch.

Ask anyone in this position, and they'll share their truth: hope is lost when your future looks less bright than your present or past. That's not thriving; that's surviving.

Step 1, Reflect, was about recognizing that you're not on track and need to start making changes. The next step will show you that you're not alone and that you should surround yourself with the people you need in your life to make those changes happen.

4

STEP 2: RELY

Teamwork makes the dream work! Nobody ever succeeds alone. (The umpteenth cliché in this book, I know.)

Money is certainly not a topic many people openly discuss. We live in a culture where silence is the dominating sound in chatter about one's finances. It's a shame. If you want diet tips, recipes, or the best deal for a lawnmower, people are happy to ask for help and share recommendations. Not when it comes to money, however.

On the one hand, we all need advice. On the other hand, many of us may have gone through a bad experience with advisers. Believe it or not, there are some bad apples in the bunch.

So what do most of us do? We go it alone. We try to be our own advisers. Just like we go to Google to help us diagnose a symptom instead of our doctor, we do the same ridiculous thing with our finances.

We need to stop this behaviour. We need to rely on the right people and trust them to help us achieve our goals. There are amazing and talented professionals who can help us get what we want and make our lives better. Choosing to be your own consultant isn't fair to you, and it isn't fair to them. When you bring the right people into your life at the right time, you'll wonder how you ever got by without them.

Going back to the concept of leverage from an earlier chapter: outsourcing the things you're not best at is a form of leverage. You win, and they win.

We agree that investment in real estate is where you need to focus. Most of us won't consider real estate a viable option over mutual funds in our RRSP because we think real estate ownership isn't easy. We settle for inferior investments because we think they're easier for us. And we want easy.

We can simplify our lives when we have the right people to help. I ask that you be open to believing this: owning investment real estate can be nearly as simple as ownership of any other investment.

Your next step is to identify the people you need to find to ensure that you are headed in the right direction.

MORTGAGE BROKER

Most novice investors skip this step. They think a mortgage has to come from their bank, so there's no need to consider filling this role on your team.

Let's bring back our discussion on numbers: assuming you are buying with a 20% down payment, you'll need a partner to lend you the 80% that is the balance of the purchase price. When you're working with a mortgage broker, you're asking them to find the right lender to borrow from for each property you buy. "Right" doesn't need to mean the cheapest lender with the lowest interest rates. Sure, low interest rates help your numbers, but it's not the only thing to consider, so be careful.

Let's discuss what a mortgage broker is and how this is different from a direct lender (a.k.a. mortgage agent). When you walk into your bank branch and ask to speak to someone about obtaining a mortgage, you will speak with a mortgage agent whom the bank directly employs. This is a direct lender. They offer their own mortgage products through their own employees. Often these mortgage agents were once bank tellers, and were promoted to fill in mortgage applications, and sell mutual funds and possibly even insurance products.

In contrast, a mortgage broker is a third party who operates independently. They have access to mortgage products from dozens of lenders (often including the bank we just discussed). The best ones work in this silo full-time. They're not being pulled into other businesses. They are excellent at finding the best loans with the best lenders while working directly for you, the investor. In most cases, they get paid directly from the lender. So you, the investor, get the benefit of choice and experience (leverage!) at no cost in most cases.

If you need a specialized product, your bank likely can't offer it. Sometimes your specific situation can't fit nicely into a banker's box and kills your qualification. Your mortgage broker can help you find funding for your purchase based on what makes sense for you. There is an entire world out there for loans. Your mortgage broker is the key to opening that door. The point is your mortgage broker is a key component in determining your loan options and the viability of a purchase.

Your mortgage broker is your personal shopper for lenders. Your mortgage broker is your Tinder app concierge, analyzing the available pool of lenders. They'll swipe left over and over until they find a lender matching your needs. That's when they'll swipe right. Eventually, they get to a point where they have their right-swiped options, and they'll approach all of them on your behalf to see if they are willing to swipe right on you!

A lot goes into this decision. They'll look at your credit, assets and liabilities, and net worth, all of which is open for review at this stage. At the same time, they'll look at your employment income from the job you haven't left yet (that's covered in Step 5) and how much money you can access.

Another benefit of working with a mortgage broker: if you have questions or concerns, you have the direct phone number of a human you can call and ask. The person answering that phone knows exactly who you are and how to help. Contrast that with calling your bank's call centre and waiting in line to authenticate yourself and explain why you're calling five times in one transferred call.

REAL ESTATE BROKER

This one is near and dear to my heart because I've been a real estate broker for over seventeen years. Your real estate broker is the quarterback of the entire real estate investment process.

When you find the right real estate broker, you'll be introduced to a team with years of experience and relationship-building.

A real estate broker is your gateway to finding the right places for the right prices. Real estate agents in all corners of the globe specialize in helping clients acquire investment properties. Not all places are equal, and neither are all real estate agents. A small percentage of real estate brokers speak the investment language. Your most challenging job will be to hire for this vacancy. You will probably be 80% of the way to riches when you do. There is tremendous value in finding the right partner.

The right real estate broker is worth her weight in gold. In any other business, we would be called out for insider trading because we know the products better than the general public. We see so many details on each property, and we can analyze mountains of information that is partially inaccessible to the public. We have the advantage and experience of visiting thousands of properties because of our real estate licences. The general public can't do this the same way. Why wouldn't you tap into that by aligning yourself with your insider? It's called an advantage, and in real estate, it's fair.

People brag about going about this process without a real estate agent. They firmly believe that, by being their own real estate agent, they'll save money and access deals that agents can't. It makes no sense to me. An excellent real estate broker has her fingers on the market's pulse and available listings all the time. Avoid being shortsighted and thinking you can "out real estate agent" your real estate agent. Get back to your leverage, and make this easy on yourself.

REAL ESTATE LAWYER

In 2023, a real estate lawyer is still necessary for property acquisition. Until and unless technology provides an alternative (like
blockchain), we need humans to help us in this part of the
transaction.

Your real estate lawyer ensures that the person or company selling
the property to you has the ability and legal authority to do so.
They handle the transfer of legal ownership into your name and
the registration of your title mortgage. And they carefully explore
and explain all factors that are super specific to the property you
buy. They are also responsible for buying title insurance for you
that helps against future claims for things relating to the land and
building that may have been missed or have not yet happened.
For example, fraud has been on the rise lately in Canada. Thieves
have successfully forged identities and have managed to assume
the fraudulent identity of a homeowner and successfully sold a
home from right underneath that homeowner. Crazy to believe,
and it's happened more often than you would assume. If that same
homeowner acquired title insurance when they bought the home,
they would make a claim to their title insurance company, and
coverage would kick in and either get the original homeowner back
in their home or pay them out with a type of financial settlement.
If that homeowner did not acquire title insurance before this, they
run the risk of having no way of coming out of this frightening
scenario. Title insurance goes beyond fraud.

A lot of mistakes can be made at this stage if you're working with
the wrong person. In this world "you get what you pay for," and
no profession operates more faithfully to this saying than lawyers.
I've seen low-cost, flat-rate lawyers botch real estate transactions.

Often what happens (illegally, by the way) is that a lawyer will hand off the entire transaction to someone more junior or even a law clerk. If you're paying for a lawyer, you have the right to expect a lawyer to work on your behalf.

Alas, such is not always the case.

Real estate transactions are usually pretty routine and straight-forward. In those cases, a low-cost law firm may be all that you need to get the job done. You can't know that going in, however. That's the danger. Having the right lawyer on your team ensures that you have all the information you need at all transaction stages. You don't know what you don't know. Your lawyer knows what you need to know.

Don't cut corners trying to save $500 here; it is not worth it.

ACCOUNTANT

Getting back to after-tax dollars, having an accountant work-ing for and advising you on tax minimization strategies is super important. I'll reiterate: I understand why taxes exist and how our society benefits from deploying that tax revenue into our infra-structure, health care, education, and more. I pay much more tax than most, so I'm paying my share. If I can minimize how much I'm paying, I will – end of the story. It would help if you were thinking the same way.

The right accountant is aware of programs and elections you can implement to keep more money in your pocket. Things like depre-ciation and when to depreciate come to mind. No offence to your guy at H&R Block; I'm sure he's super sweet. But he isn't likely to be as informed as an amazing accountant who helps investment property owners make wise decisions.

Another area of expertise the right accountant can help you with is estate planning and structuring your life. They can help you to pay fewer taxes over the long run, not just this year. Everyone's situation is unique, and your solution should be unique so that you play to your strengths. The right accountant can do that for you and with you.

PROPERTY MANAGER

Most people don't realize this, but you can separate the role of "investor" from the role of "landlord" when owning an investment property. Often the same person wears both hats, which is mainly cost-related. But no rule says you need to or even that you should.

Leverage in this scenario dictates that you can hand off the daily property management responsibilities to someone else. When you find the right property manager, it'll often come with a general contractor or access to a general handyperson who is trustworthy and crafty. When the property manager identifies a deficiency, the contractor is called to bring it back in shape. Leaky toilet? Not your problem. Sure, you'll get the invoice, but it's a wonderful trade. Unless you know how to plumb or re-wire a home, you should expect to leave the work to the pros.

Most beginner investors feel that this is the one part of the team they can do without. Most beginner investors start buying locally to be their own property managers. Most times, it works out. Other times, it pushes investors out of their comfort zone and their own investment properties.

If the intent here is to treat this investment like your mutual funds (set and forget), don't discount the property manager's role in making that happen for you.

HOME INSPECTOR

This is another one of those roles that your real estate agent should be able to help you with. A home inspector is a person you'll normally call in when you've found the right place at the right price and just want to confirm some details of the home's construction.

A great home inspector can point out issues or deficiencies specific to a home. This way, you'll know what improvements are needed before buying (if you want to). At the end of a visit by a property inspector, you'll be very clear on what it is you're potentially buying and what you'll need to do over the short, mid and long term.

You'll also learn a ton about construction and systems when you sit with your inspector on a physical inspection. This bonus provides you with an education and information you can apply to your home. Not saying you should attempt to be the next Bob Villa or Mike Holmes. Still, it's great information to have when outsourcing work, just in case someone tries to take advantage of you.

INVESTING PARTNER

Your investing partner will help you turn the equity you have accumulated in your real estate holdings into regular deposits into your bank account. This role doesn't need to be filled until you are at Step 5 of the Replace Method.

When we build enough wealth with real estate, we want to convert it to something that can replace our regular paycheques. Our investing partner does that for us. The skillset required to build wealth differs from the skills needed to retain and use wealth.

Real estate ownership is going to help fast-track your equity gains. As you'll see in the next step of the Replace Method, we're working toward creating a regular stream of income or cash flows to help you replace the need for your salary. It may come in the rent payments you'll be collecting or from the gains you'll be making in your real estate investments and using to buy cash flows. I'm preparing you to magically turn a huge pile of money into regularly scheduled paydays.

Your investing partner is the person on your team who can help you turn one into the other. Akin to a financial planner, but not the kind we've already discussed.

The skills required to *build* wealth are not the same ones learned to help *keep* that wealth. It's important never to forget that. Your investing partner is coming on board to help you keep the wealth that your previous partners helped you create. They will work to turn that large equity you've built into a steady income stream.

Recently, I realized that I had accumulated $500,000 in equity through a single real estate investment. I had built the equity. I didn't want the exposure to more up-and-down real estate cycles for this specific investment, so I chose to preserve that equity and use it for a different goal. My investing partner has the knowl-edge and network to find investment options that will take my $500,000 and apply it toward an interest-paying investment. The investment was a short-term loan with the possibility of extension, and the deal paid prime, plus 12%, which is handsome for me. That one partner helped me turn $500,000 into a steady monthly income of $6,250 (or $75,000 annually). Through the help of this partner, I traded real estate for cash flow. This final piece of the puzzle brought me close to replacing my salary. The right mon-ey-person makes all the effort in the Replace Method worthwhile.

We'll revisit this in Step 5: Replace Your Salary or Repeat Until You Do.

INSURANCE BROKER

Your next property purchase is going to require an insurance policy. It will be a requirement from your lender. If they're going to be lending you all of that money, they want to be sure that it is insured. It's a fair request, in my opinion.

You could shop around online and try to compare insurance prod-ucts and premiums. What's the deductible here, and what are the coverage limits there? Although this sounds like a thrilling endeavour, you are much better suited to bringing in someone who knows these concepts better than you.

An insurance broker operates much like a mortgage broker because they can access many insurance companies and prod-ucts. They assess the property and your ownership structure and make the right recommendations for coverage.

Trust me, looking for insurance on a multi-family home is not easy. You'll be transferred from one call centre to another and will likely be told that the company you called won't offer you insurance. You'll lose hours of your life unnecessarily. Leave this to the professionals and feel better about using your time wisely.

SUMMARY

The right team opens up a whole new world of opportunities and possibilities. When you surround yourself with the right people aligned with your goals, you will start to see so much more for yourself (and others) than you ever thought you would. Trust me. It's the most beautiful thing. Leverage is the key to opening all of this up.

Use leverage almost everywhere; it's the key to growing and scaling up. Leverage the "doing," don't ever leverage the "understanding."

Actively seeking the right people to join your team is paramount to all this work. Get referrals from others who have used some of these people and reach out. Make a connection. Find the right fit.

Finding the right real estate broker is a way to fast-track the team selection if you're in a pinch. However, it's best for you to go through the process and build your own team to surround yourself with hand-picked talent.

The right people on your team will set you up with a healthy foundation. You'll experience fewer issues by leveraging their knowledge leading up to the buy. They are an excellent source of future opportunities.

5

STEP 3: REACT

This is the most challenging part of the process. Until this point, decisions haven't really had consequences, and they've been easier to make. However, just as we defined risk as having both good and bad possible outcomes, consequences can also be good and bad. A result of finding the right life partner may have meant that you're now married, right? Kind of like that. Let's be fair and honest about this part of the process. The consequence of finally making that investment property purchase should be that you have found a way to replace your salary with passive income from this decision in a few years. That's a possible/likely consequence. If your mind is going right to "OMG! I can lose all of my money!", you need to reimagine how this will set you up for a great retirement and a better future than your present.

Once you settle down and regain your focus on the goal and commit to its achievement, you're ready. Commit to buying your first or next income property. Believe in yourself and your team. Know that you aren't reinventing the wheel; you are following through on a wealth-building plan. You are not a trailblazer. You're going to be fine. Real estate is the only asset class of significance that banks will happily lend 80% (or more) toward. They are confident in real estate holding its value and appreciating above all other asset classes. So rest assured, you are headed in the right direction.

By following this Replace Method, you will eliminate a lot of uncertainty. In anxious times, productive actions remove anxiety. Stay on track and be confident. You will need to make some decisions and learn to accept them.

You'll have to get over it if you don't like making decisions. Deciding not to decide is also a decision, by the way. So if you're a decision-avoider, know that you are still deciding by not deciding. Don't let yourself do that. Make that promise to yourself right here, right now.

PREPARE FINANCES FOR DEPLOYMENT

If you are not financially secure, you can't do the deal. In other words, prepare for the financial decision you will make. You'll need to have at least 20% of the price of the property you're buying as your down payment. The first part of your down payment, we'll call that the deposit, needs to be ready to be accessed in as little as a few hours. This changes depending on your local market. Budget the first 5% of that 20% for your deposit and have it ready to be deployed.

Note: most jurisdictions will impose an acquisition tax called a "Land Transfer Tax" in Canada. It's not applied evenly across the country, so there's no way to generalize this. Some areas charge more than others, which should be considered in your planning.

For simplicity, in this book, land transfer taxes will not be included in calculations. In your research and planning, add them as part of your down payment number to give you a clearer picture.

If you don't think you're financially ready to purchase property, call your mortgage broker to chat about what you need to get pre-approved for a mortgage. Do this now. When things are foggy, they clear up after this phase. If you've not thought about the price of the property you will be buying yet, you will get that guidance now. You may want a property at $2,000,000; however, if your mortgage broker tells you that your qualification is around $400,000, that is where you will be shopping and buying.

If you're buying a property at $500,000, you'll need $100,000 for your down payment plus closing costs to close the transaction. You can expect that you'll need that money between thirty and ninety days after finding the property. In many markets, you need 5% of the purchase price (the deposit) upfront when offering to buy a property. Again, this deposit is the first part of your down payment. Don't worry; this money isn't at risk. Your deposit will be held in a trust account at the listing brokerage's office or with a law firm. The seller can't touch this money until the purchase is complete and you get your keys.

If you're one step ahead, you've realized that there's a missing piece here. If the place costs $500,000 and you've put $100,000 toward that, what happens to the $400,000? That's your mortgage amount. That's the leverage. Your mortgage broker fits this piece into your puzzle for you.

SHOPPING FOR REAL ESTATE

With your mortgage pre-approval in hand, you likely have the blessing of a lender-partner ready to pay for the property you are about to purchase.

The natural question is: what should I be looking for?

Start with your budget. If you know you can afford to buy a $400,000 property, then make that your limit. For others, maybe that number is $2,000,000. This decision isn't up to us; it's determined by what we just discovered during our chats with our mortgage broker. Let's continue to assume your purchase limit is $500,000. This would likely directly translate into the fact that you have $100,000 as a down payment handy (plus closing costs). Perfect, then that's where you should start your search.

Next, identify the location(s) you are confident buying in. Do some research into market dynamics. I would start to look in a location with a higher population and better access to the type of tenant you want in your property. Of course, large cities will provide that. They also come with a higher price tag. What's most important to me is that I would need an area where the population is growing. If a town is losing people, homes will sit vacant. When that happens, supply picks up, and prices fall without a matching housing demand increase. Plain and simple. That's not a winning strategy.

I started investing in Toronto because I lived in Toronto. Most of us follow that pattern. As a stronger investor, I've certainly opened up to other markets from coast to coast. It's a pretty standard tale in my world. Ultimately, if you have the right team supporting you, it shouldn't matter where you own.

Start researching online. Want a hack? Government pages list numerous infrastructure projects in areas they are planning for growth. Suppose the government is backing development, highways, or transit hubs. In that case, they're probably anticipating population growth nearby – this is a great way to learn about places you may have overlooked.

If you need an example, search "A Place to Grow Ontario" in your web browser, and you'll come across Ontario's official plan for expansion. If you're stuck for ideas, this may get your brainstorming muscles in motion.

Once you've determined possible areas in which to own, it's time to loop a real estate broker back in to make this next part happen. She will see that the right people from your team in Step 2 are involved to ensure you're doing the right thing. She'll also be able to help you understand market dynamics in that region. If you've chosen the wrong area, it will be clear when you get access to market data in this phase of the plan.

Are prices falling? What are rents like? Is there an area of town that's more desirable (and more rentable) than others? Based on a reasonable purchase price and using expected rents, what do my numbers look like here? There are entire books and courses on how to analyze expenses for a property. Your real estate broker can coach you on specific property selections.

I'm pretty sure every real estate investing book ever written starts out with the same selection criteria. It's fairly straightforward – buy for cash flow. This means you should only consider buying properties with revenues (rent, in this case) that match or exceed all expenses. When that happens, the property "carries" itself.

All things being equal, this is a wonderful strategy in principle. However, it's not always achievable in larger markets where properties are priced proportionately higher than rents. In mega markets, the relationship between rents and purchase prices doesn't work as well. For example, $3,000 in rent might get you a large house in a smaller town in exchange for $400,000 in the purchase price. But in a big city, $3,000 in rent may only get you a condo that will cost you $750,000 to own. As an investor, you'll face this choice during your shopping phase. Making plenty of money in cash flow isn't always possible, but it's still something you should strive for as you set about your search.

Let's put this another way. Each area will have its market prices for rent and ownership. You can safely assume that you won't be getting wonderful results in appreciation in places where you'll make excellent cash flow. The same holds for the opposite. In markets where you can reasonably expect great appreciation, you can expect to have awful, or even negative, cash flow per month. Investors use both of these strategies. Your job is to decide which direction you want to go with your investment.

Suppose you follow the books and head for greater cash flow at the expense of appreciation. In that case, you'll be taking the safer route in general. Your income property will take care of itself. It would build up a reserve fund in time if you wanted it to. And it will pay itself down surely and steadily.

On the flip side, if you decided to pass on the excellent cash flow option and opted for the risk of the appreciation, you could reasonably expect to come out ahead over the years. You may lose some sleep and need to contribute some of your own money if your monthly rent doesn't cover all the expenses. In doing so, you would expect appreciation gains to be more significant and in a tax-preferential category.

Either way, you will come out as the winner and be significantly ahead of where you are right now.

TIMING THE MARKET

Far too often, you'll read about timing the market in online forums, where everyone seems to think they're experts on real estate investing. Things like "I'll wait for prices to fall before I buy." As if they can predict when that will happen. The market will have had to turn upwards for you to know it was at the bottom! At that point, you couldn't buy at the bottom, and you'll compete with other buyers eager to get into the market before they feel priced out.

This whole concept is called "timing the market" by Reddit and Twitter keyboard warriors.

In the great book *Millionaire Real Estate Investor*, author Gary Keller has a different take on timing the market:

"Most people think timing is about active observation – sitting on the sidelines waiting for the moment when they should jump in and take action. It's a passive and then active approach. In other words, timing is about being reactive to opportunity. The truth, however, is that timing is all about being active – active all the time. Timing isn't about being in the right place at the right time; it's about being in the right place all the time."

Going back to Step 2: Rely, be careful from whom you take advice. Don't rely on an anonymous Twitter or Reddit user in his basement to spew negativity in your direction, all in the name of getting more "likes" or "upticks" on their complaint platforms. We're better than that, and we see the good opportunities when we're abundance-minded and not scarcity-focused.

THE FOUR C'S OF SUCCESS

Dan Sullivan of Strategic Coach has built a massive business that helps entrepreneurs excel. I've not participated directly in his programs, so I can't endorse the brand. However, I know quite a few students of Dan Sullivan's, and I have come to absorb some incredible content Dan has created.

Dan observed and documented this concept of the four C's of success that operates in a repeating cycle. It's a concept that simplifies how the human mind determines and achieves success.

Here's how I understand how the four C's of success apply to us:

1. **Commitment:** change starts when we make something new a part of our life. We need to commit to making that change. Commitment starts the process toward positive change.
2. **Courage:** once we have committed to change, we must follow through. We must step out of our shells and do something that makes us uncomfortable if we expect to see new results.
3. **Capability:** now that we've found the courage to work toward that positive change, we are building skills and

getting better at the exact thing we set out to achieve.

4. **Confidence:** we crush our goals. We set a target, are intentional about achieving success and direct our energy toward getting better in the very thing that produces the results we want. We now have the confidence to own the assignment. We can even teach it! And we can make a new commitment to getting deeper and deeper knowledge and understanding of this new world we've uncovered. That starts by jumping back up to point number one with this new element we want to incorporate before restarting the cycle.

Think back to when you learned how to drive. First, you committed to putting in the time behind the wheel. It took courage to do something you've never done before. You knew you'd face panic and doubt. Still, you had to find the nerve to jump in the driver's seat and face that fear. In time, your practice made you a better driver. You were adding a new talent or capability to your resume. With that capability, you found confidence in driving. The fear is gone now, and you know what you're doing while driving. Perhaps your next goal is to learn how to race. That would take a new commitment, followed by some more courage. You see how this works.

DECIDE TO DECIDE

The whole decision process is something that fascinates me. To share my thoughts on this, I'd like to share a story with you.

I do a lot of my best thinking when showering or driving. For someone with a great computational brain and an awful hard drive (memory), many of my brilliant ideas never survive the shower or the drive.

I just came out of a drive where I spent some time remembering a recent experience when I bought skis. I learned real lessons from that process. I realized that all decisions are made once we have done "enough" research to satisfy ourselves. The study gives us the confidence to act and influences how we decide.

Let me walk you through my recent ski purchase, and you'll see what I mean and how it applies to EVERYTHING!

I was heading out to the Rocky Mountains (pre-COVID) to ski. I was a snowboarder and decided I wanted to get back into skiing. I didn't want to rent, so I decided to buy. That was step one.

The next step was to head to the ski shop, check out skis, and compare features and prices. Not being a fan of retail, I enjoyed no part of this. I am great, though, at making decisions.

Being a true leverage fan, I rely on others to do the things I don't want to do. In this case, I outsourced the research, the comparison, the pricing, and the sizing. I only wanted to get involved when it came time to walk to the cashier to buy and take the skis with me. Whatever those skis were.

The sales rep helping me was probably a minimum-wage employee. He saw that I didn't know enough to decide on my own. So I took his advice. On everything. The ski length, the type of ski, the colour and price, the boots and the poles. You name it.

I bought it all on the spot.

I trusted the sales rep with my wallet. Looking back, I had to decide if I cared enough to learn about all of this stuff myself or if I was going to trust someone who convinced me he knew more about what I needed than I did. He took over the research and selection part for me, and clearly, I was fine with that.

The research had to be done, so I outsourced it.

I'll never really know if what I bought was the right or the wrong thing for me. And here's the thing: I don't care! I don't live in regret that way, ever.

I decided. I made my choice back then. You will never hear me say, "I wish I..." because I don't live there.

I learned about myself and other humans and how we decide. This is how I see things working across any decision (yes, including big real estate decisions):

- When we set out to do something new, we want to learn about it first.
- The bigger the stakes, the more time we spend learning and researching.
- Researching goes on and on, at our own pace, in scale with the cost of the decision. The higher the stakes, the longer the decision.
- When we know enough, we should decide so that we can move on and start enjoying it, and then focus on our next decision.
- If we stay in research mode too long, at some point, we become indecisive. And this is where there are diminishing returns. The classic "over-thinking" pushes us too far,

and we can't return. We've spent so much time thinking about it that if we make the wrong choice now, it'll be a total disaster! Yikes! When this happens, the safest decision is not to decide. You can't make the wrong decision if you don't make one.

Keeping it simple, if I had to point to one thing above all else in creating personal wealth financially, it's the fact that I decide. I make decisions. Right or wrong, I never beat myself up, and I'm right far more than wrong. You will be, too.

I look at all the reasons why I should do something, sure. And, of course, I look at why I should NOT. I won't spend all my time in the "NOT" category, thereby missing or losing an opportunity – because that's what happens. I refuse to spend more time figuring out why something great may fall apart when I know it's more likely that all the good things I've learned about will make my life better.

Yes, of course, sometimes I'll be wrong. We all will. If you make a clear decision, and you've looked at the good and the bad, I think it's important to stop yourself from looking for reasons why you shouldn't when you should. Or worse, being indecisive.

SUMMARY

It's natural and predictable that making big decisions like the ones in this chapter can eventually lead to the infamous feeling of buyer's remorse. Could you have waited longer? Is there a better investment that you'll have to pass on? Am I ready for this? Maybe. Maybe not.

Don't let your monkey brain take over and prevent you from growing. You've faced big decisions in the past and have likely had great results from making big decisions. If you're married, you faced a similar decision when exchanging your "I dos," right?

For the record, you've also faced the same dilemma in small decisions. When you buy a pair of shoes, you're passing on all the others you could have bought. You realize at some point that it wasn't *what* you bought, so long as you had something protecting your feet.

I realize that buying shoes isn't the same as buying an income property, of course. In all honesty, though, it's important that you don't over-emphasize the importance of the property you're acquiring. *Time in* the market will always beat *timing* the market.

If you keep doing what you're doing, you'll keep getting what you're getting. Trust yourself, trust the steps and trust your team.

Don't wait to buy real estate. Buy real estate and wait. The best time to plant a tree was twenty years ago; the next best time is right now. So go bravely into the battle and start building that wealth so you can exchange it for freedom!

6

STEP 4: REVIEW

You've now owned your income property for a while. Hooray! I bet it wasn't nearly as bad as you thought it would be. Some of you may have even forgotten you owned property – that's how hands-off it's been. For others, you may have had to do a bit of massaging to get it to where you needed it to be.

It's time to take a step back, assess what you have achieved, and course correct if needed.

Every year, you should review the progress and the equity gains you've made from the property. Always go back to the categories we covered earlier in this book and analyze them through that lens. You'll be amazed at where you are.

A common error real estate investors make is that they somehow forget to look at the results altogether. Often in setting up the bank account where rent payments come in, and expenses come out, the investor thinks the gains made from that property directly reflect the bank balance. Don't do that! If you remember from an earlier chapter, that balance will indicate the money coming in from the cash flow. This balance doesn't reflect accumulated wealth through principal paydown and property appreciation.

Every once in a while, I'll make check-in calls to see how clients are doing with their investments. We all need to be reassured of our gains, though they are often forgotten for the reason discussed in the preceding paragraph.

Your results are NOT reflected in the bank balance for your rental property. That's only a part of it. As this is the most visible component for real estate investors, let's start with a review of how you would likely have progressed in the ideal first few years.

We will assess the three categories of wealth creation individually and then merge them for a complete analysis. Let's start with cash flow, review principal paydown, and finish by looking at appreciation numbers.

REVIEW CASH FLOW: CATEGORY ONE OF THREE

Cash flow is the money left over when you take your rental income and subtract the costs associated with owning and operating the property. Revenue minus expenses. Here's a table I use in my research. For this example, I assume a $500,000 purchase and a $400,000 mortgage at 5% amortized over thirty years.

It's not massive, but if bought under these assumptions, this property would generate a positive cash flow of $25.24 per month. This scenario includes a 5% property management fee. If this property is a condo near you, perhaps you would take on the role of property manager if that's something you would like to do.

CATEGORY	AMOUNT ($)	TOTAL ($)
Revenue		
Rent	2,550.00	2,550.00
Expenses		
Monthly Payment (5%, 30 yr am)	2,134.76	
Property taxes	250.00	
Insurance	30.00	
Property management	110.00	
Total		2,524.76
Net cash flow		$25.24

Table 1: Cash flow analysis

If you're reading this and you're thinking: "What about repairs, or that new fridge, or hydro rates increasing?" you're letting yourself focus on the small stuff. That kind of thinking will prevent you from pouncing on all of the great rewards. Of course, life will throw obstacles your way. You can't predict everything all the time. Don't let that stop you. If you choose to do nothing because you can't predict every outcome in advance, you'll end up with nothing. Focus on all the good, and don't get in your own way. Have faith in what you're doing.

Do me another favour, please. Pay yourself that property manager fee if you don't outsource it so that you get used to expensing it. You will grow, have more properties, and need help.

Let's go one step deeper with the cash flow analysis, just so you're clear on what this analysis is and is not. As described above, the way to interpret cash flow is to imagine money in your pocket. Your tenant pays you money, and it goes into your pocket. Your lender asks for some, the insurance company would like some, and you pay that from the rent you collected. Whatever is left over, if there is any, is your net cash flow.

As far as the CRA is concerned, that's not how they work their accounting. They want to see your earnings laid out in an Income Statement chart. It looks very similar to the one we just built, with one main exception.

We discussed earlier how mortgage payments are split between interest and principal amounts. Suppose we pay $1,000 toward that mortgage. In that case, it could be that $750 will pay the lender interest, and $250 will be applied to paying down the actual loan amount or principal. For the CRA, the portion of the mortgage payment that went toward the principal is not something you can list in your expenses.

When creating your Income Statement for the CRA, the net result is that you will show a more considerable gain. If you can't increase your expenses, the number you subtract from will be higher. It's straight math.

Keep this in mind when you get to that time of year when you file your taxes. The CRA blends the cash flow and the gain you have made in the next section (principal pay down) each year to account for the gains you make. They want their share of your income. It's inevitable. Death and taxes, right?

REVIEW PRINCIPAL PAYDOWN: CATEGORY TWO OF THREE

We touched on the principal paydown in the prior section. Now it's time to look at the actual results from this category. We're going to closely examine the amount of principal we are paying down each year, which is directly related to the increase in our equity. Using the same assumptions from the previous table, you can run the math on an online mortgage calculator to determine how much you would pay on your loan by the year.

In this case, we're starting with a mortgage of $400,000 when we buy. Here's what that looks like over the next few years:

END OF YEAR	CUMULATIVE PRINCIPAL PAID DOWN ($)	LOAN REMAINING ($)
1	5,956	394,044
2	12,214	387,786
3	18,789	381,211
4	25,696	374,304
5	32,953	367,047

Table 2: 5-year principal pay down analysis

Notice how the amount paid down each year increases. This is how mortgages are designed. The longer you hold the property, the faster you'll pay down the existing loan. Each year has results that are better than the previous.

Cumulatively, you have paid $32,953 toward your principal over the five years. You now have that much less to pay off your loan. If you sold, you could expect to be able to turn that into cash because you would have to pay the lender back just the outstanding amount. That's one of your options. You'll have other options, which are explained later in the book.

Restating for effect: this category of equity gain is *guaranteed* as long as you make your mortgage payments. And you will, or rather, your tenant will.

REVIEW APPRECIATION: CATEGORY THREE OF THREE

Suppose we've done a great job selecting a location where we can invest. In that case, we can reasonably expect the property value to increase each year. In my city of Toronto, historically, annual property price appreciation rates hover around 7% – 8% per year. Some years I've witnessed a nearly 20% annual increase, and I've also seen outlying years where the number was negative. Down years don't often happen, though they are possible.

We have to try to smooth out the annual increase in value so we can make some projections. Years with a 20% price increase are absurd and atypical, as are years with price drops. These are blips that historically don't have long-staying power. I want to be a bit conservative in this discussion, and I would like to use 5% as our assumption for annual appreciation.

What does 5% annual appreciation look like on a chart? Glad you asked!

This category is most likely to bring in the more significant numbers quickly. Five years with 5% annual appreciation turns into a large number. A figure of $500,000 can quickly become $638,140.

END OF YEAR	PRICE ($)	GAIN FROM PURCHASE ($)
1	525,000.00	25,000.00
2	551,250.00	51,250.00
3	578,812.50	78,812.50
4	607,753.13	107,753.13
5	638,140.78	138,140.78

Table 3: 5-year property appreciation analysis

After five years, adding up each year of appreciation of 5%, you'll gain $138,141. That's more than double what you invested. Celebrate that win.

REVIEW ALL OF YOUR NUMBERS BY MERGING ALL CATEGORIES

Remember how we discussed risk earlier? The appreciation category provides for risk, which we defined earlier as uncertainty. We aren't certain about 5% or 8%. So, yes, there is some risk to what we can expect regarding the appreciation category of income in real estate. The risk isn't *bad*; it's just *uncertain*.

In practice, the other two categories generally carry next to zero risk (again, uncertainty). Let's see if you agree after the next couple of paragraphs.

If you are buying a property in good condition in an area that you are confident needs rental housing stock, and you're going to rent it at market rent, there is a terribly small chance it will sit empty and untenanted. You can always rent under market value if you need to fill the space. In my opinion, the risk of carrying a vacant rental property is not a real risk. I'm honest about my expectations, and I've never considered this a real danger for properties I acquire. This risk is reduced when you're smart about what and where you buy.

Of course, if there's no vacancy in the rental property, we can take the tenant's rent cheques and pay them toward our mortgage. Suppose all we do is reduce our monthly loan, which is the same as increasing our equity or net worth. If we make these regular mortgage payments, this category is guaranteed.

In total, given the assumptions we made in this example and using $100,000 as your investment for this $500,000 property, here's how you'll be growing in your first year:

CATEGORY	AMOUNT ($)
Investment	100,000
Cash flow	303
Principal paydown	5,956
Appreciation	25,000
Total equity gained	31,259

Nobody should ever buy a property with such a short time horizon. The shorter the time horizon, the more unnecessary risk you take. Suppose you are looking to get rich quickly using this strategy. In that case, you can refer to yourself as a speculator or a gambler. I don't advise that plan. Looking at the gains in five years is far more helpful.

CATEGORY	AMOUNT ($)
Investment	100,000
Cash flow (with no rent increase)	1,514
Principal paydown	32,953
Appreciation	138,141
Total equity gained	**172,608**

DOUBLE YOUR INVESTMENT IN LESS THAN FIVE YEARS

Making over $172,000 on an investment of $100,000 is a stable investment vehicle. Having multiple sources of equity gain is a sweet deal. It's well over double. It's closer to triple in this scenario! Again, this is why well over 90% of the world's millionaires built their wealth through real estate.

Of course, you can't accurately predict that you'll achieve these exact results. You may have results that exceed these. You may see double or triple returns even quicker. It's also possible that it will take more time than expected.

You likely won't get rich quick, but you will get rich slowly. Trust the process, and know your numbers. The results will show up in due time. Real estate operates in cycles; when prices aren't up, remember that they will come back soon enough. As a real estate investment property owner, you are positioned to capitalize, and you will reap the rewards of your investments.

SUMMARY

This chapter was about growth and building asset values. It was also about reviewing your numbers to stay ahead. Remember to schedule a time to review your assets at least annually.

You're not going to just keep holding the real estate and living off the same cash flow forever. You'll have earned enough at some point to cover your expenses or initial investment, and then it's time to reap the fruit from the bounty you've created.

When you're holding real estate as an investment, the only number you see daily is from cash flow. That number will be small. That doesn't mean all your numbers are small. Make sure you consider all categories of equity and income.

Reviewing what's happened with the properties you own and the markets in which you own them will help you truly understand what you've accomplished toward creating massive personal wealth.

Your real estate broker will be able to provide you with market value estimates, so you don't need to do any thinking. Your mortgage statement will tell you how much principal you've paid down. If you're filing your taxes annually (and you really should, by the way), you will also have the cash flow numbers handy.

In a nutshell, you can create your financial future by thoroughly analyzing your results.

7

STEP 5: REPLACE YOUR SALARY OR REPEAT UNTIL YOU DO

This is where the magic happens, my friends. This is where the strategy, the effort and the time to grow all contribute toward the happiest of endings.

Remember the "Choose Your Own Adventure" series of books from the 70s and 80s? Well, I do. It was a lovely and entertaining way to forge your path in a book. You'd read a few pages, get to a decision point, and then take action based on that decision. When confronted with a dragon on page 77, you had to decide if you would fight (continue to page 46) or run (turn to page 96). This stage is similar to that.

Back in Step 3: React, you had to make your first big decision for Steps 4 and 5 to exist, and it took courage and faith to overcome that hurdle. You may have been timid or scared, and you had to learn how to be comfortable with being uncomfortable. In this step, Replace, you get to realize the rewards. Let's unpack your choices.

HI THERE, WHAT'S YOUR NUMBER?

This is an easy question to ask and sometimes a tough one to answer. You must find your "number" to track your targets. How much monthly income do you want to replace? Will you need more than your current salary? Or can you stop working and live on less? Think of it as your freedom number.

If your goal is to have your monthly expenses covered in perpetuity, then do the math and look at all of your expenses. Add them up, including your mortgage and property taxes (or rent), car payments, mobile phone and internet bills, utility charges and insurance. If you feel good about finding a way to earn that number each month passively, are you happy? Do you need or want more?

Whatever that number is for you, own it. Then set out to achieve it. Decide to have it!

If this is your first time reading through *Replace Your Salary with Real Estate*, you likely have not yet solidified your number, and that's fine. You'll get there. It may take a couple of cycles through this book to figure it out.

When I started, my number was $20,000 in monthly income for my wife and I. That's how much salary we wanted to replace every month with passive income. That number has changed (up and down) over the years, though it has given us a target to work toward.

If we fast-forward five years from now and look at your results, will you have created a system that has entirely replaced your salary? Have you hit your number? In the following section, I will show you how to turn your real estate wealth into regular and predictable monthly bank deposits. If it sounds like a game, it's because it is like a game.

Your goal is to know how much money you need to feel true independence and happiness in your own life. Make that number your target. I play a game with my kids called "Cash Flow" that was created by Robert Kiyosaki. It probably is the best board game around to teach financial literacy, by the way. It's clear as day when you play that game that the goal is to have all of your expenses covered by income that is not earned through employment. If your living expenses are $5,000 per month (include housing, food, vacations, utilities, etc.), then that can be your target. When you've hit your target, you've successfully replaced your salary! If you aren't quite there yet, do not fret; you'll repeat this cycle one more time and assess after that second iteration. You may need to repeat steps one through five around four or five times to get there (if you have super aggressive goals)! Focus on your personal goal, and you will arrive at your destination.

A LOOK AHEAD: FIVE YEARS LATER

Let's put all of the knowledge together and start making some projections. We've worked with one example up to this point: the single-family buy-and-hold strategy. Now that we're getting wiser, let's introduce another scenario to ensure we understand real estate laws and how they work in our favour. The fundamentals haven't changed; we're just going to change the actual investment by paying a little more to acquire a home with three apartments. In the multi-family residential investing world, it's commonly called a triplex.

Assumptions:
- You are buying a triplex property for $1,000,000, and the goal is to hold for at least five years.
- The down payment is 20%, or $200,000. For simplicity, closing costs are not considered here. They vary from province to province and from country to country.
- We are obtaining a mortgage for $800,000 at 4.89% amortized over 30 years. The monthly payment is $4,217.13.
- The rents total up to $5,250 per month, and tenants pay utilities.
- The property is appreciating an average of 6% per year for five years.
- Annual property taxes are $5,000, and insurance is $3,000. With mortgage, taxes and insurance, monthly expenses total $4,884.
- Let's loop back to our three ways of making money to see where we are five years after we acquired this income property.

1. Cash Flow

Do you remember how to calculate this? Of course you do! Cash flow is the metric we find when subtracting our expenses (costs of doing business) from our revenues (in this case, rents). Our net cash flow, in this case, is positive by $366 per month ($5,250 to $4,884).

That $366 monthly net cash flow is equivalent to $4,392 in annual dollars in one year. If you own this asset and do nothing to change these numbers, you've earned $21,960 in net cash flow. In real life, you will be raising rent annually (as allowed by law). This net cash flow number should increase if you are a prudent investor.

Results in five years: $21,960 growth in equity.

2. Principal Paydown

I love this category. Again, as long as all we do is make our payments, this equity build up is guaranteed.

In the first year, the paydown is $12,145. Remember, mortgage payments are made of interest and principal (this is what we mean by "amortized"). As we make monthly payments, our outstanding principal is reduced. As that is reduced, so are the interest dollars that our lender is making from us. The first payment is the worst and gets progressively better with each payment.

After five years of regularly making payments on this specific mortgage, we've paid down $67,044 of the outstanding loan. What used to be an $800,000 loan is now $732,956.

Results in five years: $67,044 growth in equity.

3. Appreciation

This is the most straightforward math to calculate. It's also the most gratifying. At the end of the first year, and again, assuming a 6% appreciation in this real estate market, the triplex we bought for $1,000,000 is now worth $1,060,000. That's a $60,000 increase in the first year just in this tax-friendly category.

If we continue to hold this asset and let it compound, the value of this same property with 6% annual growth at the end of the fifth year is $1,338,226. If you're a bit unfamiliar with the lovely concept of compounding, this is how it all works:

The property valued at $1,000,000 appreciates 6% in year one.

That means the value at the end of year one is $1,060,000. The property's starting position in the second year is now $1,060,000. So when that property appreciates at 6% in the second year, it's appreciating 6% from $1,060,000. That value at the end of the second year is now $1,123,600. And so on. Eventually, at the end of the fifth year, this asset is worth $1,338,226 and climbing.

Results in five years: $338,226 growth in equity.

This is what compounding does and why buy-and-hold is the best investment in real estate. Albert Einstein, the genius of all geniuses, once famously said, "Compound interest is the eighth wonder of the world. He who understands it earns it; he who doesn't pays it."

If you're doing the math and grabbing a tally of earnings here, you'll see that given these assumptions, in five years, equity growth totals $427,230 ($21,960 + $67,044 + $338,226). This is *on top* of your down payment: in this case, $200,000. If you've done all you wanted, you can reap the rewards. Cash out, take your $627,230 in five years, and use it as you see fit. You will need to keep some to pay your income taxes, don't forget.

Most of the money will be tax-preferred if our laws remain the same. The $200,000 down payment comes back to you without any tax exposure. The $338,226 in capital gains are taxed at 50%, so only half of that, $169,113, is added to your income. The other $169,113 will join your $200,000 as a tax-free pull. You would have had to deal with income tax on the smaller two categories over the year, so liability won't be significant when you sell.

Deciding to put that down payment to work five years ago has now put you in a position to afford the bigger home, maybe a cottage, or perhaps pay for university for your kids. You didn't need to lock your money into an RRSP or RESP to get the results you set out to achieve, and you did it in a fraction of the time. If you accomplished what you needed to with the plan, I wish you all the best in the next phase of your life! If you're still very much wanting to replace your salary indefinitely, you're welcome to follow one of the next paths.

REPLACE YOUR SALARY

Full disclosure: generally, I wouldn't say I like talking about retiring. You're not un-serviceable just because you're ready to stop working. The term doesn't fit perfectly. I prefer to think of it as more of a goal marker that tells you that you've reached financial independence for the rest of your life.

Retirement is a period that we all hope we get to enjoy. It's the ultimate end game. It's a lot of taking money with a lot less earning money. The earning doesn't necessarily need to stop; however, the trading of our time for that money should. If you are approaching this stage, you'll need regular payments hitting your bank account to live an amazing life. How can we use this strategy to help?

You would have two options if the goal were to fund the rest of your life. For either scenario, you must bring down your "number" from this chapter to see where you land.

1. **Turn rent into cash flow – if cash flow is higher than your "number."**
   If rents are increasing and you're starting to see excellent cash flow, you are winning! What you've just created is a

perfect retirement fund. Why? You will continue to take cash from the surplus (rent vs expenses) and have not stopped the immense upside potential still up for grabs. If the real estate cycle brings you into a down market, you won't notice. You're making enough off monthly cash flow. Meanwhile, the property will continue to appreciate. Your tenants will continue to pay down what you owe. By holding on to the property, you haven't created a sale or disposition, and so there won't be taxes owing on the capital gain. This is truly winning.

Finally, saving the best for last, as you take money from this asset in cash flows, you're doing nothing to diminish the equity you have here. Taking $5,000 in rent does not negatively affect the value of the property whatsoever. It's still being paid down or increasing in value.

2. **Sell the property to buy assets that will generate cash – if cash flow is lower than your "number" and can be swapped for an amount above your number.**
   If rents aren't giving you what you need to live well in your later years, use the sale of the property to invest in income-producing assets.

If you look around, you'll find fantastic options that regularly pay you 10% to 15% per year in interest in exchange for holding on to your funds. Trust me; options out there will provide this with minimal risk. Return to Step 2: Rely, and your team will find these options for you.

Suppose you place the $627,230 in equity in a financial instrument like this, earning 12%. In that case, you'll generate over $75,000 per year in interest or dividend payments directly to you. You likely won't have $627,230 after taxes. When you sell, you will have to pay taxes on gains. Much of the gain you would have made in the five years leading up to this would be subject to taxes.

If you're left with $450,000 after tax, for example, and you've found your way to earn 12% interest on that $450,000, your annual interest income would be $54,000. Does that number work for you? If you've hit your goal, congrats! You'll continue to earn this annually if you follow this plan. Resist the urge to take more significant amounts so you won't have to deplete the $450,000 you have in equity.

If the number you come up with when analyzing your new annual income isn't enough to give you what you want in retirement, repeat the Replace Method.

REPEAT

I want to frame this option better, as it sets the stage for absolute freedom. Let's loop back my pal Albert Einstein here and bring his love for compounding into the discussion. What if there was a way to replicate this success and amplify its results?

The results you have achieved when you're at this step will likely blow you away. It's natural to suggest that you should just do it again, right? I mean, why not? If time is on your side and you see a bigger life for yourself today than when you first picked up this book, why wouldn't you allow yourself to grow into that bigger life?

If you agree and want to learn how to double or triple these results, keep reading. If you're pleased with what you've achieved and found happiness in this journey, you can put the book down and enjoy the calm of your newfound freedom.

Still here? I'm glad we're on the same page. Let's blow this all up and compound the heck out of this. It's you, me, and Einstein here now. We'll use the same example so I don't confuse you with multiple scenarios. Just so you do not have to flip back and forth, here's what we assumed and here are the results:

ASSUMPTIONS	RESULTS AT THE END OF FIVE YEARS
• Bought property for $1,000,000. • The down payment is $200,000. • Mortgage of $800,000 at 4.89% amortized over 30 years. • The monthly payment is $4,217.13. • Rents are $5,250 per month. • The average appreciation is 6% per year for five years. • Annual property taxes are $5,000, and insurance is $3,000. With mortgage, taxes and insurance, monthly expenses total $4,884 for the first five years.	• $21,960 from cash flow. • $67,044 in loan paid down. • $338,226 in appreciation. • Total equity (including the $200,000 down payment) is $627,230. • The new property value is $1,338,226. • The mortgage remaining is $732,956.

Imagine being at the end of year five. The property is worth $1,338,226 and has a mortgage outstanding of $732,956. The equity in this property (the difference between its value and the loan) is $605,270. This is all contributing to your net worth. Enjoy that for a second.

How do you use your money to make more money? Glad you asked. You're thinking more like a true investor and less like a salaried employee.

At the end of year five, your goal is to refinance the property. That means that you'll replace your existing mortgage with a new one. Why? That's how you'll access the money you want to use to make even more.

We will use the same assumptions in the table above for this refinance. Rates may have moved up or down in the five years. We obviously can't predict, though it's fair to use the same assumptions when looking into the future.

The goal is to obtain a new mortgage on a property valued at $1,338,226. If the rules haven't changed, you'll apply for the maximum amount of loan (80%). In this case, that equates to $1,070,581. Yes, the goal is to find a lender to provide a mortgage of $1,070,581 to replace the one that got you started initially at $800,000.

Going back to your team from Step 2, you'll first engage your mortgage broker and let them know your intent to refinance the property. They'll be able to handle the logistics for you to acquire this.

If you're successful in doing this, I hope it jumps out at you that you've pulled more money from this property than what you originally bought it for! It costs you $1,000,000 (yes, plus closing costs), and you've just applied to withdraw $1,070,581. You get to keep the asset, and the equity that remains in the property is $267,645 (20% of $1,338,226)!

A few years back, you bought a house for $1,000,000. You used $200,000 of your own money to acquire it. You waited, and five years later, you got your money back (plus more), kept the house with equity of over $250k, *and* the house continues to appreciate.

When you secure that new mortgage, you'll end up with a cheque for $1,070,581, less $732,956 (the old mortgage you are replacing). How much is that? It's $337,625.

That's your equity. What do you do with that leftover money? The correct answer here is to follow the Replace Method and repeat this by doing this again! And maybe again!

SUMMARY

The beauty of this entire system is that it is repeatable. It's the tried and true method of building wealth. What you've discovered in this book is just how accessible it can be.

We all have limiting beliefs. We've all told ourselves that we "can't." Somehow we've convinced ourselves that we aren't capable of achieving great results, that we're not great people.

I'm no brighter than anyone reading this book. I've not invented anything new, in full disclosure. I just chose to see possibilities and decided to take action on opportunities. That alone is the sole reason I've been able to replace my salary with real estate.

Investing in real estate to accomplish life goals is not new. When you have the discipline to follow this process a few times over, you'll wonder why you didn't jump in sooner. You may even be upset with your former self for denying the fulfillment of knowing that money will never be a problem for you again.

If I'm being frank, replacing my salary or helping you replace your salary with real estate is not meaningful by itself. Replacing your salary lets you think bigger, knowing that you've met your financial needs and obligations. When you free up that part of your life, you unlock an entirely new you that's escaped the mundaneness and vicious cycle of living paycheque to paycheque.

In my introspection, I've found that building relationships with people who can help me reach my goals is the best way to live. Instead of thinking, "How do I access the equity in my house?" I've started asking, "Whom do I need to ask for help accessing the equity in my house?" Instead of asking, "How can I get across town to make this appointment and still be back in time to pick up my child?" I can ask, "Whom can I call to help with this appointment so I can be back in time to pick up my child?"

If you're feeling stuck, and don't feel like you have what you need to achieve your goals, remember to lean on the people around you.

Maybe I can be your "who" by having written this book. I'm happy to assume that role. If you're thinking about the different people in your life who can help you get to where you're going, you're well on your way. Your future will be a lot brighter than you've ever imagined.

PART THREE:

THE WRAP-UP

8

FREEDOM

At the beginning of this book, I promised that it wasn't a money book. There are plenty of concepts that involve money. However, money is the tool to achieve the freedom and independence we seek. Let's be honest; everything we do needs money. We've accepted that. We don't need to work a nine-to-five job we hate for the rest of our lives to fund the rest of our lives. You are more than your email signature.

I sincerely hope this book has helped you change your mindset and open your thinking up to a world that includes a bigger you. The steps and investments you make today can bring that change.

Can you imagine if, in five or ten years, when you send your emails out to a business associate that your signature reads:

....

"Currently, out of the office."
JANE SMITH
PRESIDENT OF BEACH AND A BOOK
CEO OF CHILLING AND RELAXING

....

That's a lot more intriguing of a title for your next social outing. You're sure to be the guest of honour with all that attention – if you decide you want to go! That's freedom, baby – freedom of time, money and relationships. You choose what you want to do, when you want to do it, and with whom.

You still may need to visit your weird uncle from time to time. This book can't help you with that. Sorry.

I've had some beautiful moments in my life. I married an incredible woman, the love of my life, in 2007, with all of our friends and family around. I witnessed the birth of both of my daughters. I have tremendous family and friends in my circle who are always around in good times and in bad. We were fortunate enough to be able to build our beautiful family home in the community we want to live in. I'm surrounded by wonderful people in the businesses I've chosen to start or be part of.

All of that is amazing, truly amazing.

GOOD FOR YOU, GREAT FOR EVERYONE

This may sound like a bit of a stretch, but there are benefits for others when you replace your salary with real estate.

I am critical of taxation as it is applied in Canada. In fact, I've never met anyone in my life that feels as though they are paying too little tax. I guess that means that from my own poll, everyone is critical of our taxation laws. One of the reasons we are heavily taxed and will be taxed even more in future has to do with our aging population, social security and pensions.

It's been documented that Canadians are living longer than ever thanks to medical advancements. The boomer generation has begun entering retirement and the number of retirees will grow and grow and grow.

If you find a way to sort out your own finances for your future, you won't need to rely on government assistance. The only way our government can pay for that is through higher taxation on everyone else, which is a losing formula. This isn't a quick fix, though it most certainly can be a fix. With more of us creating financial independence, we reduce our need for governments to step in and that benefits everyone.

Another way society wins when you find your financial independence is in making way for the next generation to start earning. When we're out earning decent to great salaries in our jobs, we're getting in the way of others that could occupy those positions. If they can't get the experience they need, our children or our nephews and nieces won't get a decent shot at making their own way toward a successful career. By replacing our salary needs with the lessons from this book, we will vacate some of the office chairs that can be filled by these same people.

If we figure out our finances for ourselves, we allow them to figure out theirs for themselves. We both win.

It seems a bit existential and lofty. I won't dispute that. Does it seem impossible as an outcome? It doesn't, right? There are benefits across the board when we implement the structures laid out in *Replace Your Salary with Real Estate.*

YOUR NEXT STEPS

I'm hopeful you are thinking bigger than you were before you picked this book up. Sometimes, all we need is a little push to nudge us into a bit of a different path than the one we were settling for. If someone gave you this book and the contents of the preceding chapters have made you feel inspired to make some amazing changes in your life, I hope you appreciate what that friend has done for you. My suggestion: pay it forward and do the same for someone else.

Remember that anonymous colleague I mentioned from Chapter 1? Well, I like to imagine an alternative world where this book made its way back through time and into his hands. I see him in my mind's eye, happy and healthy, and leaving the office on his terms because of the lessons he learned from this book before his company removed him from his office. I let my imagination stay in that vision from time to time, to remind me that there is someone out there just like him who could use a bit of help and education – much like he needed. I'd like to find ways to share the power of independence and freedom with that person. That person may also be you.

This book discussed a lot of concepts surrounding money, yet it is most definitely not meant to be a money book. It's a freedom book. Achieving a larger bank balance was never what inspired me to live this way; rather, it was the freedom of time, of money, and of relationships that having a larger bank balance would be able to provide.

You decided to read this book because something was calling you to seek out change in the way you're conducting your personal financial affairs. The way you've been getting by simply isn't going to cut it long term.

Replace Your Salary with Real Estate started out by identifying the two ways one can earn money in this life: trading your time for money (job) and trading your money for more money (investing). The vast majority of people only live in the first category, and they'll always have a limit or a ceiling to what they can do. It's only when you embrace investing that you begin to scale, and you'll allow yourself to continue to earn money regardless of whether you show up for work or not.

The key for this strategy is in the 5-step Replace Method.

1. Reflect – look at your finances, compare to your goals
2. Rely – build a team and play to their strengths
3. React – believe in yourself and have courage
4. Review – set regular intervals to assess your results
5. Replace Your Salary or Repeat Until You Do – convert your real estate gains into a steady stream of money that exceeds your income

None of what is proposed here is rocket science, and none of this is ground-breaking or cutting edge. All of these techniques have been used by many investors and at many stages. The way that I've incorporated this into my own life and into the lives of my clients allows us to be super clear on what our goals and objectives are.

When I'm out looking for my next acquisition, I know without a doubt what my objectives for that property are. I have a plan, on the way in, to eventually convert/sell that property when it reaches a certain value so that I can turn that into steady cash deposits into my account.

I was interviewed for the "3 Pillars of Success" podcast recently and the host, Geraldine, asked me how I determine success. Some may define success as all the riches in the world and all the shiny objects that come along with that. My answer wasn't as glamorous. I said I value balance and having "enough." I love working and I don't want to miss my kids as they grow up. I value time with my wife. I love travelling and exploring. I love building businesses. I need balance to be successful. I can't go all work and I can't go all fun. I need a blend of both. Taking away the burden of needing a salary makes this all possible.

I don't need too much, and neither will you if you really think about it. What's your "enough"? It's really simple. If you follow this book as a guide, you'll find "enough."

I'm excited for your upcoming journey and I hope that you share all your wonderful stories with me! I expect to compile a journal of amazing results that are created from readers of this book, and I'm thrilled to have participated in making the change in your life.

MY FAVOURITE MOMENT

I want to share my all-time favourite memory from my recent personal history.

My wife and I regularly travel on group trips with friends and our children. We do this with different friendship groups; we're that lucky. One of those trips was an end-of-school-year trip for two weeks to Italy. We spent the first week in Tuscany, where we rented this gorgeous villa at the top of a small mountain overlooking the town and the sea. Sounds spectacular, I know. FYI: it wasn't any more expensive than a week in Mexico at a resort, though that's neither here nor there.

I remember this vividly. I sat on a patio after eating dinner al fresco (outdoors). I was holding a glass of Italian red wine and listening to the chatter and laughter all around me from the beauty of this vantage point. The kids had their bathing suits on and splashed around in the pool. It was La Dolce Vita; the good life.

As I sat and enjoyed the moment, my iPhone beeped. I ignored it. A couple of minutes later, another beep. A few seconds later comes another beep. I have a fantastic team back home that is more capable than me at handling what needs to be addressed at work. I wondered, do they need me for something? I'm not one to ignore responsibilities, so I checked the notifications, pulling out my iPhone out to see what all of this was about.

There were four messages of direct deposits into my account from my tenants. It was the first of the month; I had forgotten. While I was out doing what I dreamed of, the universe started sending me income. The things I had done leading up to this moment put me in a position to receive those emails.

With all due respect to my amazing wife and lovely children, this was the best moment in my life – this was freedom. Since I grabbed it, I haven't let go.

Thank you for reading *Replace Your Salary with Real Estate*.

Please share your story with me via email at donny@teammangos.com. I promise to read each one.

Here's to your success!

GET IN TOUCH

🌐 replaceyoursalary.ca

📷 replaceyoursalary.ca

📘 page is "Replace Your Salary with Real Estate"

📘 private community group for people looking to collaborate and participate "Replace Your Salary with Real Estate"

✉ donny@teammangos.com

ACKNOWLEDGEMENTS

A lot of people have had impact and influence on my life and my book. I'm fortunate to have sought out and found some wonderful humans, who were around to listen, to chat, to offer advice and to play devil's advocate.

First and foremost, in typical cliché fashion, I do want to thank my wife, Catherine, for her love and support. I am messy and confusing and definitely struggle with shiny object syndrome. All of that cannot be easy to live with. Catherine has been the most stable thing in my life. She and my daughters have been my reason for wanting to build and make a dent in the world. My family is entirely my "why." If I was missing this part of my life, I likely would settle for a lot less. Thank you for being my reason.

To my parents and family: I know we came from humble beginnings and we didn't have much. Heck, we didn't even speak English for the first four years of my life! We had to learn as we went, and we all did the best we could. It's because of you that I live within my means and I appreciate the value of the dollar and its impact on my life. My father was the one who encouraged me to acquire my very first property at the age of twenty-two, when other dads likely would not have. The result of that one decision shaped me forever.

To Jamie Purvis: you put on a perfect demonstration of perseverance and integrity going back to the very first time we met. You, unknowingly at first, took on the role of being my mentor. You had me set that $20,000 monthly goal that forced me to be honest with myself. I owe that "sliding-doors" moment to you. Thank you.

To Tuan Tran: the way you assessed, analyzed and communicated how you see investing in real estate turned on a switch in my mind. It's because of that day in our office when you blessed me with the gift of your time that I was able to eventually turn my vision into a plan, and now a book. I have told you many times that you are a legend. Thank you.

To Trisha Enriquez: when I asked a favour of you to help be a reader of an early version of this book, you immediately agreed. Your feedback directly influenced some of the content. When I sat down to write this book, you and Emil had tons of mindshare in my brain. I kept you both there as I typed, knowing that it was people just like you who I wanted to be able to help. Not that you need help! Thank you.

To Colin Rivers: just like Trisha, I thought of you and Miyuki often when I planned this. Unknowingly, you helped shape the contents of this book as well! Your detailed and critical mind helped sharpen these pages up. You're constantly thinking three levels deeper, and it truly helped me understand the audience and their questions more clearly.

To my extended family, Bill and Gina and Gus and Claudette: going back years and years here, you've been with me and my family every step of the way. It's for friendships like this that Catherine and I want the freedom of time. Spending every weekend together in the winter and looping in Trisha and Emil every summer for "chosen family" vacations makes life much sweeter. Thank you.